War Between
Russia and China

Books by Harrison E. Salisbury

HARRISON E. SALISBURY

War Between Russia and China

W · W · NORTON & COMPANY · INC · New York

FIRST EDITION

SBN   393   05394   6

Library of Congress Catalog Card No. 70-96828

Published simultaneously in Canada
by George J. McLeod Limited, Toronto

The map and key on pages 132–33 were taken from *Territorial Claims in the Sino-Soviet Conflict: Documents and Analysis* by Dennis J. Doolin (Stanford: The Hoover Institution, Stanford University, 1965).

All photographs, with the exception of the one from Sovfoto, were taken by the author or his wife, Charlotte Y. Salisbury.

PRINTED IN THE UNITED STATES OF AMERICA

1   2   3   4   5   6   7   8   9   0

For Juan and Allty and
Beth and Silas

Contents

Photographs will be found following page 96

Foreword

This book has been written out of concern over the tension between Russia and China and the proliferation of signs that the two superstates are headed toward a collision course and war. I do not share the complacency of those who view the prospect of such conflict with equanimity or even hopeful anticipation. Russia and China not only are superpowers; they are nuclear superpowers. War between Russia and China will be nuclear war. Even if we escape direct involvement—which seems most dubious—we could not escape the fallout. Should the blitzkrieg which Russia's generals promise the Kremlin succeed we would be confronted with a new Communist colossus in which the Soviet Union commanded the joint resources of Russia's industry and technology and China's population. If Russia's generals fail to make good a quick knock-out of China the prospect looms for a grinding conflict which might dominate the international scene for the rest of the century or longer. No man can now foretell the fateful repercussions of Asian continental war.

The United States can profoundly influence this struggle and will be profoundly influenced by it. We occupy a position of leverage. We are linked with neither contender. Our power can be employed to insure Russia's victory, to insure China's victory, or to prevent Asian armageddon. By employing our superior weight and influence we can transform impending disaster into the foundation of a new and stable world structure. It is to that objective that this work is dedicated.

War Between
Russia and China

CHAPTER I

The Hinge of
the Earth

The road to Kara Korum lies across the open steppe. From whatever direction you approach the broad plain where the black hundreds of Genghis Khan once camped and where in 1235 his grandson, Ugedi, erected the magnificent capital that Genghis planned but did not live to see, you traverse the endless grassy plateaus of central Mongolia.

The first time I came to Kara Korum the month was June. The steppe was green and verdant; the scent of the *aiga*, or Asian fennel, was strong in the air; slow flocks of sheep were moving up to the higher mountain pasture; and the ancient Mongol capital appeared over the horizon like a giant conjuring trick, the 108 small *stupas* of the Buddhist shrine of Erendi Dzu rising symmetrically in a sea of green like some Asian Stonehenge.

There was an air of peace and solitude about Kara Korum when I saw it a decade ago. It stood alone and isolated on the steppe. Not far distant was the Kara Korum State Farm, a hopeful hostage of the future. Here with Russia's guidance the Mongol herdsmen had been displaced. The bountiful grasslands had been put to the plow. Wheat was being planted. The land was being watered by an irrigation system installed by the Chinese. Signs of Russian-Chinese conflict already were visible elsewhere but here at Kara Korum stood an active testimonial to the friendship and collaboration of the two great Communist powers and their remote, small (but strategic) associate.

In May of 1969 I again set out for Kara Korum. The steppe was as I remembered, rolling, eroded, and endless. But now, before the June rains, it was gray and brown instead of emerald. The jeeps headed out over the roadless plain, following the hard-beaten trails that horses' hooves had engraved before the day of Genghis Khan.

We had not driven fifteen minutes before a huge brown cloud filled the sky and darkened the sun. Presently the cloud passed and the sun shone feebly; then another cloud, low and menacing, appeared. The clouds were dust—dust from the furrowed lands, the virgin steppe ravaged by twenty-gang plows working across the broad valleys, almost invisible within cocoons of gray, pulverized earth. The wind was strong—forty to fifty miles an hour—and it lifted the earth particles in spectacular whirlwinds that rose thousands of feet into the air. The *purga*, straight from the Gobi, chilled me to the bone. But it was not the cold which froze my attention; it was the spectacle of the Mongolian earth, the remarkable steppe which had nourished a hundred generations of horsemen, going straight up into the air in sheet erosion to rival that of the Oklahoma dustbowl.

I felt that I was witnessing a kind of Wagnerian tragedy, a drama in which the small and fragile figure of a man was being overwhelmed by protean forces, set in motion by the human but mindless idea that we could improve the balance of nature by putting the plow to the ageless grasslands.

This brooding sense of elements, uncontrolled and uncontrollable, overhangs the Asian heartland today—not only Mongolia, but the expanses of Siberia, the deserts of Central Asia, the forest and riverlands of the Soviet Maritime provinces, and, so far as one can judge from a distance, the remote forbidden regions of Inner Mongolia, Tibet, Manchuria, North China, and the ancient caravan routes of Sinkiang.

But it is not the winds of the Gobi, the Pandora's box of nature, ripped open by man's brutal assault on the steppe, which has touched off the syndrome of apprehension.

The urgent, overpowering question dominating the Asian heartland today is simpler, older, more terrible. It is: Will there be war between Russia and China, war that would set Asia aflame, war whose nuclear winds would poison Gobi desert, Manchurian plain, China riceland, and Siberian taiga alike, turning a supercontinent, if not the world, into a hostile environment in which even primitive life might no longer be supported?

The fears of the peoples of inner Asia may seem overdramatic, remote, or unreal to those who have not seen the changes of the past decade. But to the nomadic herdsman who watches complex and mysterious electronic devices being installed in the mountains east of Ulan Bator, to the frontier guards who fight sudden savage battles along the Ussuri, or to the worried villagers who each night listen to the eastward pounding of long supply trains on the Trans-Siberian or hear the rumble of truck caravans rolling south from Ulan-Ude, from Chita, from Blagoveshchensk, the menace is real and immediate.

Nowhere is this more evident, more obvious than in Mongolia.

Long since the collaboration of the Russians and the Chinese has ended in Mongolia. There are no Chinese helping to maintain the irrigation works on the Tarany River serving the Kara Korum State Farm today. You will look in vain in Mongolia for any mass of Chinese; a few plasterers, desultorily refurbishing a remote hot-springs resort; four or five painters ironically assigned to decorate the welcoming arch at the gates of Ulan Bator for the state visit of Soviet President Podgorny; a plumber to put in order the drains of the British Embassy (a house built by Japanese prisoners of war and formerly occupied by the Cuban Mission, which decamped Ulan Bator rather than pay the high rent imposed by the Mongols)—these are the remnant of 40,000 Chinese laborers once suppied to Mongolia free of all cost, with China paying their wages, subsistence, and transportation as evidence of her friendship.

Long since the Chinese teams which erected most of the big government buildings and apartment houses in central Ulan Bator have been sent back home, not a few of them barred by police and security troops from construction sites before the buildings were finished. (Some of the buildings still stand, gaunt, incomplete, boarded-up, monuments to the hostility which touches every relationship with China.) Gone is the Chinese acupuncturist, the doctor of the thousand needles from the Ulan Bator hospital. Gone, too, are the Chinese acrobats from the circus.

One clause of the agreement under which China supplied her labor force to Mongolia provided that any Chinese had the option of taking Mongol citizenship and settling on the land. It was a device by which the Chinese might have introduced into Mongolia a massive Fifth Column. But not a single Chinese has opted for Mongol citizenship, or if he has he has been so "discouraged" that he has gone back to China.

Ten years ago the Chinese labor battalions in uniforms of blue proudly marched with their Mongol comrades in the great Naadam national-day parade. Today a handful of Chinese remains in Ulan Bator and looks out on the scene from behind the great walls of the enormous embassy compound—as big as any the Great Powers of Europe once maintained in Peking. The Chinese are invited to ceremonial meetings but quickly and demonstratively walk out as Mongol orators inveigh against the "great power chauvinism of the clique of Mao Tse-tung."

Ten years ago the young students at Ulan Bator University yearned to go to Peking not just to complete their education but to imbibe the spirit of the "true Asian revolution." There existed among the Mongol intellectuals strong sympathy for China. There was a pro-Chinese faction in the Mongol Communist Party. Mongols openly argued whether they should follow the Russian or the Chinese path to communism. Not a few believed that given a free option China would be Mongolia's choice.

Long since every hint of pro-Chinese sentiment has been ruthlessly stamped out. No students go to Peking today. None would dare publicly express such a desire—if he felt it. Even Chinese-language studies have been abolished at the university—no longer any need for them, the Vice Rector explains. A few Mongol intellectuals who sympathized with China and chanced to be in Peking when the split came have remained there. If they returned home they would face the concentration camp. The pro-China faction has been weeded out of the Mongol Communist Party. No Party orator today speaks in public without incorporating a denunciation of Peking in his text. In place of praise for their Chinese friends and thanks for their help the Mongols now excoriate—with specifics of time, place, and circumstance—Chinese efforts to subvert their regime, to violate their frontiers, to conspire against Premier Tsedenbal, to commit acts of treason, treachery, and harassment.

Ten years ago, before China and Russia had by public word or deed indicated the slightest break in official friendship, in the solidarity of Communist comradeship, in the firmness of the military and economic alliance, it was in Mongolia that symptoms of the great Communist schism were discovered. Here in the depths of Asia, far from prying eyes of outsiders, in a land so remote that few Europeans or Americans could precisely locate and bound its frontiers, the evidences of the split were exposed—

openly hostile remarks by Russians against Chinese and Chinese against Russians; intense conflict between the two powers for dominant influence with the Mongols; rival and competitive aid programs; aggressive campaigns for political and propaganda influence within the Mongol intelligentsia as well as within the upper echelons of the Mongolian Communist Party.

There were visible in Mongolia in 1959 all the traditional aspects of Great Power conflict and rivalry. But these great powers, as bewildered Americans still point out, were those supposed true and eternal partners of communism, Russia and China.

It is no accident that it was precisely in Mongolia that the cutting edge of the Soviet-Chinese dispute first became visible and that it is here in Mongolia that the Russian-Chinese conflict has advanced farthest in preparation for open warfare.

Mongolia may be remote geographically from the Western world, but it fulfills a strategic function which belies its isolation. One need not accept the worn and dubious concepts of geopolitics to understand Mongolia's critical role. It is what Sir Halford J. Mackinder, the founder of geopolitical thinking, would have called a true "geographical pivot of history."

Mongolia is the heart of the Asian continent. Thus when, due to a combination of circumstances (the organizing ability of Genghis Khan, a cycle of favorable weather, the resulting improvement of the Mongolian pastures, the increase in fodder and a sharp rise in the nomadic herds of horses), the Mongols launched their military campaigns in the twelfth century they succeeded within a half century in conquering most of the known world. They were located at the gateways to the great Asian empires. They could—and did—sweep southeast into China. They could—and did—sweep west to conquer the decaying emirates of Central Asia. They swept south from Central Asia into India and southwest into Persia. They moved north to ravage the wastes of Siberia and west across the level deserts and plains into the even greater plains of Russia. Only when they reached the very threshold of Central Europe did they find themselves too extended for primitive and nomadic forms of organization and supply.

Genghis Khan, his sons, and his chiefs were only following fairly well-worn paths earlier traced by the Huns, the Visigoths, the little-known Scythians, and others.

It was Mackinder's theory, rather grandiloquently expressed, that "who rules the Heartland commands the World Island; who rules the World Island commands the world." The location of the "heartland" was a matter on which he was not always precise. In 1918, at the end of World War I when the rise of communism in Russia deeply alarmed him, he placed the "heartland" in East Europe. But a more familiar location was deep in Asia—the locale of the Huns, of Genghis Khan, of the Manchus, of the Russian-British struggle on the approaches to India in the nineteenth century, and of today's Sino-Soviet conflict.

Mackinder spawned the school of geopolitics, a philosophy always closely associated with the imperialist or continental aspirations of one nation or another. In Germany it found expression in the theories of Karl Hausoffer, the ideological patron of the Nazis. In Japan Mackinder's thinking and his hortatory rhetoric are echoed in the famous Tanaka Memorial to the Japanese Emperor of July 25, 1927. The Tanaka Memorial is particularly interesting because although its authenticity has long been challenged it finds mention in almost every Soviet political work on East Asia and is accepted by the Russians apparently without question. As the Tanaka Memorial put it: "In order to conquer China we must first conquer Manchuria and Mongolia. In order to conquer the world we must begin by conquering China."

The fascination of the Tanaka Memorial is its pertinence to Russian and Chinese policy. If the two great Communist countries do not consciously espouse this doctrine their policies clearly reflect the same kind of thinking. The truth is that Tanaka sums up the principles which underlay Russian policy for at least a century before the Communists and the continuity of that policy with the policy of the Soviet regime in the Far East is unbroken. It is not for nothing that the Chinese are calling the men in the Kremlin "the new czars."

From the seventeenth century forward the Russians pressed east over the ill-populated reaches of the Asian continent. It was an eastward march very similar to the westward march of the United States from the Atlantic to the Pacific. In the fifteenth century the territory of the Muscovite principality had been separated by more than 2,000 miles from the farthest outposts of China's Ming empire. But over the centuries the outriders of Russia—traders and trappers, explorers and freebooters—steadily closed the gap.

As early as 1650 the Russian traders and the small companies of soldiers sent to protect them were clashing with Chinese along the Amur River. There were pitched battles and constant friction. Finally, the Treaty of Nerchinsk—the first China signed with any foreign power—was negotiated and signed in 1689. This defined the boundaries in general terms and spheres of interest. By the treaty Russia recognized China's right to the vast eastern reaches of Siberia. The dividing line was set at the watershed between the Lena and Amur River valleys, leaving the rich Amur territories clearly within China's domain.

But the treaty did not halt the Russian push. Russian explorers had reached the Bering Straits as early as 1648, and with Count Bering's explorations in 1728 the area began to be developed. Bering penetrated Alaska in 1741 and by 1784 there were Russian settlements in the western hemisphere. Russian fur traders had ranged down the Pacific coast as far south as Fort Ross, California, by the time of the War of 1812.

The main activity of the Russians, however, was in eastern Siberia. They constantly sent expeditions into the territories formally conceded to China, extending their operations into the Pacific littoral (the Maritime provinces). At the same time daring Russian military men and explorers penetrated the forbidden areas of Central Asia, a Chinese domain (with some interruptions) since the second century B.C. By the latter part of the nineteenth century Russia had gathered into its sway almost all of the lands free to be gathered north of India with the exception of Tibet. British and Russian guns frowned at each other over the weak body of Afghanistan.

The nineteenth century was the century of China's disintegration. The European powers descended on her like vultures, tearing at the limbs and torso of the dying empire. The British, the French, the Dutch, the Germans all were awaiting the kill. The Russians were there, too, possibly less conspicuous to American eyes because their pressure was from the interior of Asia, thrusting down from the Amur, seizing the rich lands of the Ussuri, planting the Russian flag at Vladivostok (Ruler of the East) in 1860—the name and site deliberately picked by the Russians to symbolize their pre-eminence on the Pacific littoral. Already they had set up powerful garrisons at Chita and Khabarovsk (named for a Russian commander). They moved in military detachments to protect their traders in distant Sinkiang province and came within a gasp of detaching the rich Ili gateway from Peking's feeble hands, being thwarted not by China but by the aroused and fearful British.

The chief emphasis, following the Tanaka principles, was always on the heartland, Mongolia and Manchuria. To Russian eyes Manchuria seemed more important at the moment; Mongolia could wait. It was then a decadent Manchu protectorate, dying under the influence of Manchu corruption and the enfeebling presence of tens of thousands of Buddhist priests. Half the men in Mongolia were drafted into priesthood and celibacy, and thus were subtracted from the manpower of the state. Mongolia, like a rotten apple, would fall into Russian hands.

Manchuria took more doing. Here the Russians moved in force. By 1898 they had compelled the Chinese to lease to them

Kwantung peninsula for twenty-five years. They built the Chinese Eastern Railroad to link their new province solidly with the Trans-Siberian, connecting via Harbin with Vladivostok. They built the South Manchurian Railroad as a shortcut to Mukden, Port Arthur, and Dairen. They began to industrialize Manchuria. Russian capital opened up Manchuria's coal mines, built her first steel mills. It was only one step more to full annexation. There was no doubt in the minds of the czarist ministers: with Manchuria added to eastern Siberia and the Maritime provinces, Russia would dominate the Far East industrially and militarily. Peking, weak and faltering, would be under the nose of the Russian guns facing down from Manchuria and the interior of Mongolia.

Russia would be the paramount power, superior to the omnipresent British and the parvenu Japanese.

The flaw in the czarist Russian blueprint only became apparent in 1905 with the shattering defeat by Japan. Russia paid the inevitable price. Not only was she compelled to cede the southern half of Sakhalin island, but she was compelled to yield her lease of Kwantung province, the South Manchurian Railroad, the great naval and industrial complex of Port Arthur and Dairen, and her dominant position in Manchuria.

Japan had already seized the Kurile islands a 1875 "at a moment when Russia was weak" (according to a recent Soviet Communist account). With her victory in the Chinese-Japanese war of 1895 she had acquired Korea and Formosa. Now by the Treaty of Portsmouth, which ended the Russo-Japanese war, Japan—again to quote a Soviet Communist historian—had succeeded in blockading "the key positions of Russia on the Pacific Ocean."

This recital of Russian imperialist objectives and her setback at the hands of Japan in 1905 may seem ancient history in the contemporary world of Communist ideology and nuclear determent.

Do not be misled.

Soviet Communist propagandists and contemporary histor-ians base themselves upon this history. Today's Soviet goals are rooted in it. You will look in vain for any measurable divergence between the objectives of Russian czarist policy in the Far East and that of today's Soviet leadership. The czarist heroes of the Japanese siege of Port Arthur are today's heroes of Communist Moscow. When Soviet forces entered Port Arthur in 1945 they knelt at the memorial to Port Arthur's defenders of 1905.

The defeat of czarist Russia in 1905 did not end Russia's drive to the east; it was merely a setback—a serious one. But Russia dreamed of revenge. She continued to pursue her aims in China and in China's sphere of influence. The next Russian chance oc-curred in 1911 when the decaying Manchu regime fell and Dr. Sun Yat-sen's Chinese Republic came into being. Russia took ad-vantage of this event to bring Mongolia within her sphere of influence. The Mongols had suffered some 200 years of Manchu domination, and it was natural for them to accept Russian assur-ances of protection for their independence. In 1911 the Mongol theocratic Bogdan Khan declared his independence of Chinese rule and was granted the protection of the Russian state. The Bogdan has long since died; the Russian czars have passed into history. Communist rule came to China two decades ago, but Mongolia is still under the protection of the Russian state, the keystone of the structure which the Soviets have erected to pre-serve, protect, and extend Russian aspirations in East Asia and the Pacific.

During the brief and restless period between World War I and World War II Russian power in the Far East was, of neces-sity, weakly exercised. From 1918 to 1921 and even later Mon-golia was a no-man's-land. For a time much of Siberia eluded Soviet grasp, becoming the domain of ephemeral White Russian regimes and the arena of foreign intervention (particularly Japa-nese). Only the presence of a token American force under the blunt, courageous General William S. Graves prevented the Japanese from detaching Siberia and the Maritime provinces from Russia and adding them to the sphere of influence which they had carved out during World War I in Manchuria and North China.

Gradually the Soviet Russians regained authority in Siberia, driving out the White Russian forces. The interventionist troops slowly fell back and ultimately were withdrawn (with the greatest of reluctance on the part of the Japanese).

But Mongolia hung in the balance, a battleground of Japanese regulars and irregulars, Chinese adventurers, the dregs of the White Russian Siberian forces, and not a few bands of sadist marauders, including that of the notorious Baron Ungern, an anti-Communist adventurer who led a wild company of mercenaries composed of Russians, Chinese, Mongolians, and Japanese through several years of skirmishing, plunder, and murder until ultimately captured and shot.

Finally in 1921, with the help of the Soviet Far Eastern army, a Mongolian nationalist Communist movement headed by Sukhe Bator won out in Mongolia but communism in the contemporary sense came very slowly. The theocratic rule of Bogdan-gegen, the Buddhist abbot-king, went on until his death with the Bogdan as the symbol and Communists exercising power in his name. But even after he died in 1926 the Communists (and the Russians) were reluctant to assert a powerful role.

Russia was still weak, although not as weak as it had been in 1919 and 1920 when Lenin demonstratively denounced the "unequal treaties" between czarist Russia and China. Nothing, in any event, came of that gesture, and by 1924 the Russians and the Chinese had made an agreement for joint operation of the Chinese Eastern Railroad that effectively retained control in Russian hands.

It was not a moment to press strongly toward traditional Russian goals. Japan was powerful, growing more so, and itching for a pretext to aggrandize itself at the expense of a weak Russia. Nor was the situation to change for some years. Japan grew stronger and stronger in North China.

With the 1930's Japan's militarists engineered the seizure of Manchuria, setting up a protectorate called Manchukuo under the puppet emperor Henry Pu-yi. The Japanese Kwantung army, more than a million strong, ruled Manchuria and North China. Relentlessly it cut away at the body of China; remorselessly it probed beyond Manchuria's frontiers. For nearly a decade before World War II Russia lived with the ever-present danger of war, declared or undeclared, with Japan.

To cope with the threat semi-independent armies were built up and stationed in the Far East—the so-called Red Banner Far Eastern Armies. The best of Russia's military commanders headed these crack forces. Their mission was war with Japan, but only if Japan forced it. Russia was not strong enough for offensive operations.

Then as now Mongolia played a central role in Russian strategy. It was the buffer which protected trans-Baikalian Siberia from direct Japanese attack. Not that Russia invested much in Mongolia; the Russians didn't seem to care whether Mongolia transformed itself into a Communist state or not. They treated it basically as a remount base for the Red Army, a source of horses, meat, and, to a minor extent, saddles, saddlery, and leather. No industries were built in Mongolia except a small meat-processing plant and a tannery. For the local citizenry the Russians contented themselves with putting in a vodka works, a brewery, and a candy factory.

Mongolia was seen as dispensable—if necessary—but more hopefully as a glacis, a shield for Russian Siberia, a field of maneuver, a zone of operations in which the Kwantung army might be extended, harassed, and brought to defeat, or at least to a halt.

The loss of Mongolia, Russia knew, would imperil Soviet

rule in the Far East, in the Maritime provinces, and in all areas east of Irkutsk. Whether Irkutsk and the Baikal region could be defended if Japan took Mongolia was uncertain. Whether Soviet rule could withstand the loss of Siberia was equally uncertain.

To both the Russians and the Japanese the 1927 Tanaka Memorial seemed accurately to state the role of Mongolia as the key to the continent.

Twice in the decade of the 1930's the Japanese military challenged the Russians in the Far East. Once the thrust was against the vulnerable Ussuri River line. Once it was more serious—a direct assault upon Mongolia. Each time Soviet forces mustered overwhelming strength to crush the Japanese. The Soviet position was clear: if Japan found any weakness in the Far East she would strike and strike again, and only by holding Japan at arm's length could Soviet hegemony be preserved.

When Mongolia is seen in the context of history any surprise that it has again assumed a critical role in great power conflict vanishes. Mongolia is a pivot stone of history, just as Mackinder described it. Today Communist China is master in China's own house. Long since the Japanese have fallen away as did the Manchus before them. But the strategic significance of Mongolia has not changed. If Russia is to be dominant in East Asia, if Vladivostok is truly to be "Ruler of the East," if Moscow's 300-year *Drang nach Osten* is to resume, Mongolia holds the critical role. Any Soviet thrust eastward and southward will inevitably be made from Mongolia. Any thrust at Chinese Communist strength—just as any thrust at Japan's Kwantung army—will be made from Mongol concentration points. The Chinese troops today stand precisely where the Japanese troops stood thirty years ago. Politics and regimes have changed. Geography has not. Mongolia's relationship to Manchuria, to the great industrial complexes founded by the Russians, developed by the Japanese, inherited and expanded by the Communist Chinese, has not changed. It is today as it was in 1938, 1939, and 1945 when the Russians and Japanese fought.

Conversely, Mongolia is as important to China as it was to Japan's Kwantung army. If the Chinese industries are to be secure in Manchuria, if the new Chinese cities in Inner Mongolia are not to be under constant threat, if the great nuclear facilities of Inner Mongolia and farther west in Kiangsu are not to stand under danger from long-range rockets, if Peking itself is not to be imperiled by a sudden double envelopment, if these basic military challenges are to be coped with with some assurance of security, Mongolia must be neutralized, at a minimum, and brought to China's side if possible.

In the view of the military, Mongolia is not merely a great empty range for horses, sheep, and cattle extending 2,000 miles from east to west, sharing a 2,500-mile frontier with China and an 1,800-mile frontier with Russia. It is not merely the historical locus of Genghis Khan and his famous hordes. It is not simply an interesting example of a nomadic people attempting through the medium of communism to find a transitional path to sedentary agriculture and industrialization. It is, as Genghis Khan once put it, "the hinge of the earth."

This would not, perhaps, be true if Russia and China were in partnership—as envisaged on paper in their treaty of February 1950, or as the world in general viewed them until recent years. It is the schism between Russia and China which has imparted this deep significance to Mongolia. What is essentially important is that when the supercontinent of Asia is in conflict, when there are two powers seeking to dominate the "world island," Mongolia becomes the key position. It was true in the days of Genghis Khan. It was true when Russia and England contested for Asian dominance. It was true when Russia and Japan collided. And it is true today with the collision of Russia and China.

None of this explains *why* Russia and China are on a collision course. That is another, more complex story. What history does make plain is why, given Soviet-Chinese conflict, Mongolia becomes the jewel in the strategic crown. When—and if—war starts between Russia and China the first shots may not be fired on the Mongol frontier. But Mongolia will hold the center role in the unfolding conflict.

CHAPTER II

The View from Russia's Side

The roots of Russian-Chinese hostility are even more tangled than those of most national quarrels, but Mongolia provides the touchstone—not today's Mongolia, but the Mongol Empire of Genghis Khan and his heirs. There were great and terrible invasions of the Russian steppe before the Golden Horde took to the Asian highroads. Russia lies like a sea of land between two continents, the compact, mountain-and-river-bounded territory of Europe and the vast expanse of Asia, secure behind the fastnesses of the greatest mountain ranges in the world. The Russian steppe is open, east and west, north and south. Time and again Russia has been invaded. No people could long inhabit such a land without acquiring a deep and suspicious outlook on the world. Who knows when a new invader might appear beyond the distant river, beyond the low rise of land to the east which marks the almost indistinguishable boundary between Asia and Europe. The Urals are no massive range like the Alps, the Himalayas, or the Caucasus. They are a low worn rank of hills, here and there marked by an outcropping of rocks or a stone escarpment, particularly along the course of the Ural River. Approaching them from west to east the traveler can hardly believe that this is the continental divide.

Peoples living as the Russians do develop a special instinct for survival. They watch the level steppe for the cloud of dust that betrays the horseman's presence as the crew of a treasure-laden galleon watched the horizon for a pirate sail.

Unless one understands the geography of Russia one cannot understand the psychology of its people, particularly the attitude of Russians toward the nomads of Asia. Russia has been invaded, in its time, by the Swedes, the Lithuanians, the Poles, the Germans (Frederick the Great as well as Hitler), the Turks, the French (Napoleon), the Finns, the Danes, the English (the Charge of the Light Brigade), and a good many others. But the great and terrible scourges came from the east. It was from the east that the Scythians appeared in prehistoric days and ravaged the fat lands along the Black Sea. It was from the east that the Huns swept in, burning and pillaging. It was from the east that the most awesome of conquerors, the Mongols, came.

Not many Russians today remember the incident at Otrar on the Sir Darya River in the summer of 1218. Not many recall Quarezum, the vast kingdom which once held sway in the middle reaches of Central Asia. Certainly no one in 1218 had any notion of the consequences when Inalchig, governor of Otrar, ordered his men to seize the 500 mules and camels of a caravan sent by an obscure Asian chief named Genghis Khan and murder its escort of a hundred traders.

It was the incident at Otrar, one of the hundreds of occasions of pillage and piracy along the dangerous caravan routes of Asia, which changed the history of Russia. Russians may not know the name of Otrar but 700 years later they still live in its shadow.

When word of the incident at Otrar reached Genghis in Peking (he already had conquered China) he swore vengeance. In the spring of 1219 the Mongol hordes gathered once again on the high plateaus around Kara Korum. They assembled in their enormous units, the hundreds, the tens of hundreds, and the hundreds of hundreds. Then they swept west, laying waste as they went. At each great and rich city of Quarezum they left a monument—a towering pile of human skulls. This was the fate of Otrar, of Turkestan, of Jand, of Beneket, of Kojend, of Bokhara, of Samarkand, of Urgench, of Nishapur, of Ray (the present-day Teheran).

Ever westward ranged the insatiable hordes. They burst into the Caucasus in 1220–21 and out onto the rich plains of Russia the next year. Soon the Mongols had swept far to the north. They reduced the fabulous Kievan dynasty, as wealthy, as advanced, as great as any in Europe, to ashes. Once the Mongols came they stayed. They sat for centuries on the backs of the Russians. The primitive Russian princes preserved themselves by "taking the yarlik," that is, by making the kowtow of allegiance to the Mongol chiefs. Moscow fell. Novgorod fell. Not for 250 years did Russia rise again, reconstitute her lands, and sweep away the Mongols. As late as Catherine II, at the time of the American Revolution, Mongols still ruled the lower Volga and in the Crimea.

This is not ancient history. It is current history. Russia still struggles against the legacy of backwardness, ignorance, servility, submissiveness, deceit, cruelty, oppression, and lies imposed by the terrible Mongols. The years have bred in Russian souls a hatred, a suspicion, a fear of eastern conquest so deep that it is ever-present, lying on the surface or just under it. Marxist ideology and Communist morality insist upon the absolute equality of races, the obliteration of chauvinism, the suppression of hatred based on race or color. But Russians render only lip service where Asians are concerned. Russian terror and Russian hatred of the peoples of yellow hue and slant eyes are too deep to be hidden. Europeans used to say: "Scratch a Russian, find a tartar." It is true that Russians possess a tartar heritage, but a more accurate aphorism would be: "Scratch a Russian, find a Russian." No Russian mother would think of permitting her daughter to marry a Mongol, a Chinese, or any non-Aryan Asian. She would have deep reservations about an Armenian or a Georgian. Not to mention a Jew. I once listened to some Russian girls argue with a friend who had fallen in love with a Kazakh movie director. He was a fine, educated, good-looking man who loved the girl deeply. He had an excellent job, a good income, and a pleasant, outgoing personality. This meant nothing to the Russian girls. To marry a Kazakh—a slant-eyed yellow Asian—was unthinkable. The girl argued for her lover but as the talk went on I could see that she was wavering. In the end she did not marry the man.

The Mongol inheritance is a part of every Russian. The historian Kluychevsky elaborated a theory to explain the persistence into the twentieth century of the oppressive authoritarianism of the Romanovs. The key, in his opinion, was the Mongol scourge. Ordinary Russians, discussing the backwardness of their country, describing the characteristics of the "dark people," as they still call the peasantry, invoke the memory of the Mongols. A provincial official, telling of the struggle to bring "culture" to a god-forsaken "bear's corner" in old Russia, will speak of the Mongols and the burden they imposed on Russia, just as his predecessor, the czarist *chinovik*, did a hundred years before. After all, says the provincial Party chief, we are two or three hundred years behind because of the Mongols.

The Mongols invaded Russia more than 700 years ago. Listening to Russians talk you might think the Mongol and other Asian incursions had happened only yesterday. Only when one is aware of the immediacy these events still possess in Russian minds does it become possible to understand the fervor of racial chauvinism displayed toward the East and its peoples.

If the question—What has this to do with Communist China? —is asked, the answer is simple. The Russian makes no distinction between the peoples of the East. They may be Uzbek, they may be Mongol, or they may be the Han people of China. To the Russian they are all the same. He does not distinguish between the Mongols who ravaged his land 600 years ago and the masses of China whom he believes are standing just beyond the low hills of Asia ready to attack again, silently, secretly, without warning.

This hereditary, racial "set" of Russians provides the environment into which must be fitted the present-day antagonisms and hostilities. It is to these historic, atavistic attitudes that contemporary events are related. When a Russian speaks of China, when a Russian says with an angry sneer that "it is time we taught these people a lesson," when he exhorts a visitor that "we Russians are Europeans, Westerners like you," he is speaking out of an emotion which sees Asia as a continent of savage warriors ready to race across the open steppe, burn his house, sack his city, and rape his women.

The poet Alexander Blok tried to epitomize the spirit of the 1917 Revolution, to capture the essence of Russia in the November days with his famous poem, "The Scythians," in which he proclaimed: "We are the Scythians . . . We are the Asiatics . . . With slanted eyes and greedy lusts . . ." He may have come close to the truth. There is a Scythian within each Russian. The Russian is a product of Asia as well as of Russia, of the invading horsemen as well as of European culture. Yet not many Russians would echo Stalin's famous phrase, uttered at the Kazan railroad station where he bid farewell to the Japanese Foreign Minister Matsuoka, on April 13, 1941, after the signing of the Russo-Japanese nonaggression pact. Stalin (who in his day certainly displayed as much fear and anti-Asian chauvinism as any of his countrymen) said, with an arm around the bewildered Japanese diplomat's shoulders: "We, too, are Asiatics." No Russian of the present generation, even from motives of political hpyocrisy, would make that statement.

A Westerner leaving Peking in the spring of 1969 was entertained at dinner by a Russian colleague. The Russian was deep in gloom. He hated Peking, hated having to stay behind. "Don't forget," the Russian warned, "we Russians are Europeans and we Europeans must stand together against the yellow hordes of Asia." He could not have realized how closely his sentiments echoed those of the late William Randolph Hearst, the great American chauvinist who for two generations sought to awaken America to the "yellow peril."

Not long before Khabarovsk was closed to foreign travel an English tourist visited the city and was given a riverboat ride on the Amur. His Russian hosts took him for a two-hour trip down the river. Finally, they said they must turn back. Why, asked the Englishman.

"Beyond that bend," said his Russian guide, "lies China."

He paused and dramatically intoned in English:

"East is East and Vest is Vest and never the twain shall meet!"

Kipling may not be the favorite English poet of the contemporary Russian generation, but he comes close to epitomizing its spirit. Yevgeny Yevtushenko, one of the more radical or unconventional of the current group of Soviet poets, has had many bouts with Soviet authority. In the last couple of years his going has become rougher and rougher as the Soviet Party line has cracked down more and more strongly against any deviation from orthodoxy. Yevtushenko had nothing published in Moscow for nearly a year, until the Ussuri River border fighting between Russia and China in the spring of 1969. Almost immediately he returned to print with a chauvinistic poem right out of the tradition of Kipling.

Said Yevtushenko in his poem, called "On the Red Snow of the Ussuri":

You can see in the murky twilight
The new Mongol warriors with bombs in their quivers
But if they attack the alarm bells will ring
And there will be more than enough fighters
For a new battle of Kulikovo.

For Yevtushenko nothing comes more naturally than the identification of Mao and the Chinese with the Mongols. To him they are the "new Mongols."

The Russian fixation on Genghis Khan seems inescapable. One indictment Soviet propagandists bring against Mao and the Peking regime is their "positive evaluation" of Genghis Khan. The Mongols, Moscow points out, wiped out no fewer than forty individual countries, bringing them under Mongol sway by war and terror. Yet Peking insists that in this process the Mongols gave their subject peoples an opportunity to lift their level of social attainment, widen their horizons, and improve their economic condition.

Apparently, commented one Soviet propagandist, the Chinese did not feel that the death of millions of people and the colossal destruction of property was too high a price to pay for an opportunity to become acquainted with "Chinese culture."

In a brochure prepared for distribution to Party agitators a Russian commentator quotes from a speech made at a Chinese Communist meeting held in 1942 in honor of the anniversary of Genghis Khan: "He created an enormous state which spanned Europe and Asia. He unified his nation and led the struggle against insults by foreigners, ceaselessly and resolutely fighting against all enemies. The success of Genghis Khan is explained by the fact that he united the people and worked together with them in happiness and in sorrow, creating a new social order and justice. Today as we honor the memory of Genghis Khan we must especially study the national spirit with which he was able to rally his people and struggle against enemies."

To this characterization the Russian writer simply appends:

"No comment is necessary." He is aware how offensive every word of praise of Genghis strikes the ears of his countrymen.

No event, international or personal, occurs on a completely blank page, a sheet of human consciousness on which nothing has been written. One reason Americans have found difficulty in interpreting Russian attitudes toward China and the Chinese is because we do not know the history and national psychology against which contemporary events must be viewed.

We do not ordinarily think of racism and racist attitudes as being characteristic of Russians. We reserve such appellations, for the most part, for ourselves and we tend to think of racism largely in black-white terms. Russians do not think of themselves as harboring racist feelings, either. They have been taught by Communist ideology and propaganda that they do not look at the world in racist terms. When they set up a provincial government in Uzbekistan, for example, and interlace Russian and Uzbek officials in such a manner that the Uzbeks hold the ceremonial offices and the Russians hold the power, they think of this as merely a kind of stewardship in which the Russians are helping the backward Uzbeks to take their first steps toward national identity.

But the truth is that Great Russians—that is, Russians whose nationality is of the principal Slav strain—traditionally have held superiority attitudes toward smaller peoples and particularly toward the peoples of Asia. One of Lenin's last complaints before succumbing to the paralysis of his final illness was against the racial chauvinism of some of his close associates, including several who themselves were of minority origin, notably Felix Dzerzhinsky, his Polish-born chief of security police; Josef Stalin, his "specialist" in nationality questions; and Sergo Orzhonikidze, who, like Stalin, was born in Georgia.

Americans, particularly in recent years, have acquired great sensitivity and awareness where racial problems are concerned. We have conducted a kind of national soul-seeking and soul-baring on the subject. We work in a thousand ways (if still far from effectively) to eradicate and minimize racial prejudice.

Nothing of the kind has been done in the Soviet Union. Party leaders simply deny that racial prejudice exists. If Russian students beat up African students because they resent seeing black Africans going out with blonde Russian girls, the government denies that the incidents occurred or blames them on Western propaganda. Russian racial prejudices, be they anti-Semitic, anti-black, or anti-yellow, are freely expressed and assumed to be "normal."

No Russian finds it unusual to hate the Chinese. He does not apologize when he says "little yellow bastards." He becomes indignant when an American suggests there is anything racially chauvinistic about his attitude. "If you had had our experience . . ." he will say sententiously. He has no notion of how similar his remarks are to those of a supporter of George Wallace talking about attitudes toward the blacks.

When Soviet specialists streamed back to Russia in 1960 and 1961 after they had been recalled from China, each had a stock of horror stories: the Chinese were stupid, uncultured, ignorant. They did not appreciate the enormous aid and help being given by Russia. They ate with chopsticks and their food was fit only for donkeys or goats—no borscht, no caviar, no vodka. Worst of all, the Chinese tried to argue with the Russians and convince them that Moscow was wrong and Peking was right; they thrust propaganda leaflets into the hands of honest Soviet engineers; they declined to accept Moscow's authority.

And they were *different*—different in color, appearance, customs, language, clothing. They did not accept the obvious superiority of Russia and Russia's ways.

We are apt to think of Russia and China as Communist countries whose history, respectively, began on November 7, 1917, in the case of Russia and October 1, 1949, in the case of China.

Nothing could be more misleading.

No Russian reacts to China in terms of a particular date or of recent events. No Russian thinks of China as simply a geographical location, inhabited by persons who (once) shared his political faith. The Russian thinks and sees China through the prism of Russian culture and history of thousands of years of fighting and war; he may not know his history accurately; he may confuse Mongol with Chinese; but the emotional attitudes fixed in his childhood and reinforced throughout his adult life condition him and color his thought. For a hundred years after Waterloo English children grew up in awe and dread of Napoleon. The memory of Alexander of Macedonia is still fresh in Iran. The image of Hitler will haunt Russia and Europe well into the twenty-first century. Unless we equate Russian psychology with this kind of trauma we cannot hope to understand why, with the advent of a powerful Chinese regime, the Russian-Chinese schism has come so close to the edge of military resolution.

CHAPTER III

The View from China's Side

I was sitting in the Harbor View Restaurant on the roof of the Mandarin Hotel in Hong Kong talking with a very earnest young Chinese. Around us soft-voiced waiters, earnest busboys, cosmopolitan captains catered to a conglomerate of New York department-store buyers, transistor tycoons, Chinese speculators, British machinery salesmen, and lady tourists from Scarsdale with or without their husbands. In an interval between the petite marmite and the langouste I asked my companion the question I have been putting to Russians and Chinese again and again for the past ten years—what was the real basis for the quarrel between the two countries, why was it so passionate, so violent, why did every effort at conciliation seem doomed to fail?

The Chinese looked at me with something between pity and contempt.

"You know our situation too well to ask that question," he said. "Look out of the windows of this hotel, which, certainly, is owned by the Americans, but I believe there is a considerable Chinese interest. From this window you see the harbor and all the shipping. You see the Chinese Communist flag a hundred times a day on passing ships and junks.

"If you could look over toward the Hilton Hotel you would see a great white building—the Shanghai and Hong Kong Banking Corporation. Next to that monument to the old China is a building just as big—the building of the Bank of China—of Communist China. Today it is covered with flags, Chinese Communist flags. As you drove through Hong Kong today you saw the Chinese Communist flag in every street. You saw it flying all the way up the mountain to the peak—from the windows of ordinary apartment houses and from the roofs of great business establishments, factories, department stores. Those flags are celebrating the end of the ninth Party Congress in Peking."

He mentioned this, he said, merely to show that while Hong Kong was still technically under the control of the British, China was omnipresent. There was no question but that Hong Kong was Chinese. The British knew this, recognized it. If it suited China to let the British, the Americans, and the other international traders stay in Hong Kong for the time being that was China's business, her own decision which she could abrogate whenever she wanted. It happened to be good business at the moment to let the foreigners remain in Hong Kong. It was worth perhaps half a billion dollars a year to China—no small sum, considering the embargo on her foreign trade imposed by both Russia and the United States (an embargo the Nixon administration is moving to "soften" in some respects).

This might be true of Hong Kong, I conceded, but what about Macao? I had been to Macao and I was puzzled by what I had found. Here was an old and corrupt Portuguese colony; I supposed it was the oldest foreign concession in China. It existed less than a stone's throw from Communist China. I had stood beside an oil-smeared creek filled with garbage, not fifty yards wide. Beside me a dump smoldered and the wind blew the heavy smoke across to new Communist China. On the Communist bank of the creek stood two Chinese Army men with their tommy guns. They came out of their sentry hut when my car stopped, peering at me standing beside the ugly shacks where refugees from their China were housed, wrinkling their noses at the stench of burning capitalist rubbish, watching steely-eyed until the car pulled off. Nor was that all. Some newspaper friends in Macao told me that the Chinese Communists held the real power in the colony although they permitted the Portuguese to continue in nominal authority.

The head of the Macao Chinese Communists was a certain Mr. Ho Ying. He was the chairman of the Macao Party, held a seat in the Communist Central Committee of China (thus demonstrating that Macao was regarded as an integral part of China), and at the time I was in Macao was off in Peking attending the ninth Party Congress. Mr. Ho was also Macao's biggest businessman and banker. He was a partner in the concession which held the gold monopoly in Macao, the cartel which was officially permitted to import gold from Hong Kong into Macao. The trade was recognized internationally and was completely legal. Gold was sent from Hong Kong by courier on the fast hydrofoils which left Hong Kong every hour on the two-hour trip to Macao. In Macao the gold was sold on the international exchange. What happened thereafter was well known but could not be proved by public record. The gold was melted down in one of the four gold smelters in Macao into "smugglers' shapes," those shapes most convenient for money belts, women's brassieres, fishing pouches, harnesses for airline stewardesses or itinerant peddlers. Off it went to the west, possibly to Laos for the international opium trade, possibly to Saigon for the heroin business, possibly to India to find its place in the secret hordes of the Indian princes. Or it might vanish into China to enter the Communist gold reserves or, more conventionally, simply be flown to Switzerland and placed in one of the famous anonymous numbered accounts in a Swiss bank.

This gold trade was Macao's most profitable source of revenue. Mr. Ho and three of his friends made their own private fortune from it. But this was not the only pie in which Mr. Ho had his fat fingers. He and two other partners held another concession from the Macao authorities, the gambling concession. They ran the three casinos in Macao, the great tourist attraction which each weekend brought thousands from Hong Kong. The casinos were the basis for the whole Macao tourist industry. There was only one other attraction of any note in Macao, the dog-racing track. Mr. Ho and the Party members did not, so far as I could learn, share in the take of the dog track.

I suggested to my hot-eyed young Chinese friend that it was difficult to understand Macao's relationship to Communist China. He smiled. Well, he said, it is not that important, but Macao is not a "concession." It is a territory allotted by the Chinese government in the seventeenth century where Portuguese traders are permitted to reside and engage in trade. The land was never alienated from China; there was no lease, no concession; sovereignty in full was preserved. This was an important distinction. Macao belonged to China and the Portuguese had never contested that. China could do anything it wished with Macao and China had never had any difficulty with the Portuguese. If China wanted to let the Portuguese stay there that was her business. If she wanted to let Mr. Ho and his friends make some money that was her affair.

All of this seemed a long way from the China-Russia dispute. But not to my Communist friend.

What you have to understand, he said, is this. Long ago all the great powers yielded their special rights, their special privileges, their territorial concessions, their unusual perquisites gained from China in the days of her great weakness. The Japanese had lost their privileges at the end of World War II. So had the Germans. The British and the French had waived their extra-territoriality, their special status as citizens, their special rights to customs, to railroads, to trade, in most cases even before the Chinese Communist regime took over. The Dutch, the Danes, and all the other Europeans had done the same. When the Chinese Communists came to power, the great cities where the foreigners had held sway came back to China—Shanghai, Canton, Hankow, Tiensien, the treaty ports, and all the rest. Hong Kong and Macao were special cases because that was what China wanted.

But this did not happen with the Russians, and this was one reason why there was so much feeling now. Russia and China in 1949 supposedly were Communist countries. They should have been working together, sharing and sharing alike. This is what China expected. But the Russians saw things differently. They still do. They did not hand over in 1949 the territories and resources which they had grabbed along with the other imperialist powers when the old empire was weak. They hung on to them. They clung to their special position in Manchuria and North China. True, they cited the danger from Japan and the United States as an excuse, but in addition they set up joint stock companies to exploit China's resources. Imagine! China had just got the international capitalists off her back, and now Moscow came along and took their place! The new companies were just like the old European capitalist concessionaires—no better, maybe worse. And these were China's Communist comrades who were exploiting her. They hung on to Port Arthur and Dairen. They hung on to the South Manchurian Railroad and even took over its links in North China. They made it very apparent that they had "special interests" in Sinkiang, the same kind of "special interests" that czarist Russia had had. They plotted with the minorities in Sinkiang and with their own colonies of Russian settlers. It was an open question whether Russia or China would win control of the territory.

Then, there were the territorial boundaries. China wanted to make a settlement of frontiers with Russia, as she had with other neighboring countries. It was true that China had not reached agreement with India and that this quarrel had led to fighting, but China did not expect such an attitude on the part of her Communist ally.

In fact, China found that Russia would not even talk about the boundary question. When the matter was raised directly by Mao Tse-tung with Nikita Khrushchev in the autumn of 1954 Khrushchev flatly declined to discuss it. Moreover, he stopped off at Khabarovsk on his way back to Moscow and made a chauvinistic speech to residents there and, on his return to Moscow, launched a campaign to organize the settlement of millions of young Russians in the eastern territories.

So, my Chinese friend went on, when we think of Russia we think of her as the last of the European exploiting countries, the one great European power which has not relinquished its special position in China, which still holds Chinese territory. We feel passionately about this. More passionately in many ways than we do about the United States for keeping Taiwan away from us. After all, the United States position in Taiwan only came about in 1950. The Russians have been encroaching on China for more than 200 years.

One did not need to know whether Mao shared all the views of his passionate young supporter to understand that from China's side the Russian quarrel was deep and broad. Into it had gone much of the chauvinism, nationalism, and xenophobia which were the natural outgrowth of the humiliating years of European domination. When the antagonism against Russia first began to bubble to the surface about ten years ago there were disorders and widespread attacks upon Russians in such cities as Mukden in Manchuria. For the most part the Russians who were attacked on the Mukden streets were not Soviet Russians but the remnant of the White Russian anti-Communist colony which had been resident there since before or just after the Bolshevik revolution. It made no difference to the Chinese mobs; the victims were Russian and they were white. Indeed, there had been in recent years innumerable incidents, particularly since the rise of the Red Guard movement, of street assaults by Chinese on white Europeans of any nationality, usually in the mistaken belief that the victims were Russian.

The Chinese carried out a comprehensive program of repatriating all foreigners resident there at the time of the Communist takeover. Within a few years virtually all Europeans had been sent home, usually at their own initiative. The arrests of missionaries and priests who attempted to remain persuaded almost all those remaining to get away as quickly as possible. But there was one group of foreigners which was slow to leave— the Russians. There were nearly 200,000 Russians in China in 1949, most of them anti-Communist White Russians who had lived there since the Bolshevik revolution. Many were reluctant to leave, because they had lived in China their whole lives and had no place to go—certainly not to the Russia they or their parents had fled so long ago.

Nevertheless, in the first years of the new China most Russians were gotten out of the country. By the 1960's only a few thousand were left. The Chinese went from one Russian family to another, even to Russians who lived remote from any other Russians or Chinese in the most desolate regions of Sinkiang, and urged them again and again to leave, bringing economic pressure on them, harassing them in every way. Their complaint was always the same: all the other Europeans have gone—the English, the French, the Germans. Only you Russians remain. Why don't you go home?

China had suffered the presence of domineering foreigners for a century and a half. Now she was putting her house in order. It was time for the foreigners to get out. And they did. By 1969 the United Nations refugee officials in Hong Kong estimated that fewer than 500 foreigners, largely Russian, remained in China. The foreign population of Asia's greatest nation had been reduced to something less than that of Luxembourg or Monaco.

Sometimes today's chauvinism by Chinese is equated by foreign observers with the furious attacks of the Boxer rebellion upon the Peking foreign colony or with the xenophobic violence of the opium war of the 1840's. The violence and the chauvinism is there and it feeds into and underlies Chinese attitudes toward Russia, since Russia constitutes the only foreign presence still in China.

Behind this is a philosophical and cultural posture which is hardly understood by Westerners, particularly those not familiar with China.

China historically regarded itself as the "Middle Kingdom," the kingdom between heaven and earth, not quite as high as heaven but well above the mundane earth. The Chinese Emperor was conceived of as the direct link between ordinary mortals and heaven, closer to heaven than any other being. China was surrounded by a world of barbarians; in fact, the Chinese word for "foreigner" was "barbarian." These barbarians were considered by the Chinese to be a little better, perhaps, than apes, but not of the degree of mankind. Only Chinese were human in the higher sense of the word. The Chinese did not merely assume the superiority of their civilization over other civilizations; they assumed that their civilization *was* civilization. There were no others. This concept colored all their relations with and perception of the world beyond their frontiers. China was the special bearer of culture and enlightenment to the outer world of darkness. As the Chinese Empire expanded it brought enlightenment to dark peoples. It imposed upon them its culture and gradually the barbarians became civilized, became Chinese. This happened again and again, as China saw its history, and it happened not only with the wild and formless peoples around the periphery, but occasionally when a barbarian tribe or group (like the Mongols) seized Peking they, too, with the slow passage of centuries, became Chinese.

As the bearer and guardian of culture, China never relinquished her sway over lands once they fell within her orbit. Holding this philosophy, she did not view the ambassador or emissary who came bearing gifts or tribute to the Emperor as a representative of an equal power but as the lackey of some unenlightened vassal come to bow at the celestial throne.

This, then, was the nation and these were the people who found themselves, early in the nineteenth century, falling into subjugation at the hands of the Europeans, the most barbarous of barbarians, men of different hue, men who did not even understand the principles on which civilization was built, men with arms so powerful that they could—and did—compel the civilized men of the civilized Chinese state to endure indignities worse than any the Chinese had imposed upon their lowest vassals. The Chinese had to watch their great cities taken from them. They saw their people forcibly addicted to the barbarian traffic in drugs. They stood by as their great cultural and religious monuments were dismantled and hauled off to barbarian lands. They had to submit to new ways of life and new kinds of "culture," which to their thought were not culture but the rude and ignorant habits of European ape-men. And they had to accede to the loss of control of vast segments of the empire—and none of those segments were greater in scope than those seized by the Russians.

The new regime of the Communists meant many things to the Chinese but none, perhaps, more striking than the restoration of national dignity and China's right to be master of her own house. Mao Tse-tung did not preach the restoration of ancient Chinese culture, Confucianism, Taoism, or the sacred principles which underlay the Chinese worship of their Emperor. But he did preach China's renaissance as a great nation and a great power; a nation capable of defense of its frontiers; a nation capable of redressing centuries of wrongs inflicted by foreigners and foreign powers; a nation restored to world leadership, proud, confident, and even arrogant; a nation which was not going to let old scores go unsettled.

There were many factors involved in China's border dispute with India. The conflict was not a mere quarrel over boundaries. It played a role in China's relations with Russia. India had been China's first great non-Communist friend after 1949. Chinese-Indian relations were warmer and closer than those China had with any power, including Russia. Then Moscow began to court India and India began to move away from her unilateral relationship with China into the posture of an intermediary. India's rivalry with China became more apparent. India was China's only Asian challenger for political leadership of the weaker Asian states—a powerful rival with her tradition of neutralism and her great charismatic leaders, Gandhi and Nehru. Also, many Asian nations traditionally feared China because of her size and power and long history of conflict. They did not fear India. If India could be driven from her neutralist philosophy and compelled to resort to arms like other nations; if she could be humiliated before the other powers of Asia; if she could be handicapped as an economic and political rival by being required to divert resources from social purposes to defense purposes; if she could be forced to become a member of a bloc, instead of operating as the leader of an independent "third-world force"—if all these aims could be achieved while, simultaneously, China was demonstrating to her people and to the world that she meant business as far as restoring the old frontiers was concerned—then China's war against India in the Himalayas could be made to produce major returns. There was another factor in China's calculations. Russia had become increasingly unfriendly. If Russia could be compelled openly to choose between India and China then, or so Peking must have thought, Moscow's real role in the Communist world could be revealed.

With these factors at stake, China challenged India and did so successfully. Her troops pushed forward and seized the contested regions. They still hold them, a visible demonstration to every Chinese that his government now has the strength to protect China against barbarian challenge. Even if all the other goals of the India war were not achieved, this alone made it worthwhile in Mao's calculations.

Elsewhere China did not resort to war to establish or stabilize her frontiers. She signed a frontier agreement with Pakistan—in part, at least, as an object lesson to the Indians. She made a similar agreement with Afghanistan. She negotiated a settlement with Burma (although this did not bring an end to her threatening activities on Burma's northern frontier). She agreed to a frontier with Nepal and, belatedly and in rather uncertain circumstances, signed a settlement with Mongolia. The only frontiers which, theoretically, remained unresolved were those with Laos and the Soviet Union.

The uncertain circumstances of the Mongolia situation rested on the fact that the agreement, suddenly reached and announced December 26, 1962, probably was arrived at as a chessboard move in China's rivalry with Russia over political influence in Mongolia. Since that time there have been more than a few hints from Peking that regardless of the settlement she retains her historic interest in a traditional Chinese protectorate over Mongolia. Actually, China's recognition of Mongolia's independence rests on tenuous foundations. It was extracted from Chiang Kai-shek by Stalin in 1945 as part of the price of his promise to intervene at the end of the European war against Japan. Chiang has long since repudiated this promise. There are strong indications that Mao, too, has reservations about Mongolia's independence. He has charged publicly that Mongolian "independence" is only a cover for Soviet domination.

According to some Soviet sources, when Nikita Khrushchev was in Peking in the autumn of 1954 one question Mao wanted

to discuss with him was the "liquidation of Mongolian independence." Mao took the position at that time that Mongolia
historically belonged to China, to which the Russians rejoined
that since the Mongols under Genghis conquered China they
might equally well lay claim to Peking.

The Russians contend that Mao has consistently had the
intention of re-establishing Chinese hegemony in Mongolia.
They point to a statement he made to Edgar Snow in 1936 in
which he said that once the Communists were victorious, Mongolia "automatically" of its "own free will" would become part
of the Chinese federation. He reiterated this thought in an inter-
view with Gunther Stein in 1944.

Thus, they say, his proposal to Khrushchev in 1954 was only
a natural and logical extension of a long-term intention to re-
assert Chinese domination of Mongolia. The extreme suspicion
and hostility with which Premier Tsedenbal of Mongolia views
Peking would indicate that he agrees with this view.

It is not insignificant that Mao Tse-tung and Chiang Kai-shek
appear to share the same view on most territorial questions.
There appears to be little difference in their views on Mongolia;
there was no difference in their view on the Indian frontier question; and they are even in agreement about Taiwan. Each regards
it as an integral part of mainland China. They differ, of course,
on who should control China.

Chinese propaganda sometimes seems to be equally directed
against Moscow and Washington, but a sharp distinction in
China's attitude toward Russia and toward the United States is
made in actual discussion by men like Premier Chou En-lai and
former Foreign Minister Chen Yi. Visitors come away from these
talks with a feeling that the differences between Russia and
China are differences of principle whereas those between China
and the United States are superficial and relate almost entirely
to Taiwan.

The Chinese have hinted occasionally that if the United

States indicated a willingness for change on the Taiwan question, even if it were only to recognize that Taiwan is an integral part of China and that its disposition is a question for the Chinese themselves to resolve, this would be sufficient basis on which to begin a re-evaluation of relations. But with Russia, they say, the question is more complex, basic, and difficult.

A Chinese diplomat, speaking in the spring of 1969 in Peking, said that the United States attitude toward China was, essentially, correct until the time of the Korean war—that is, up to that time even though Washington had not recognized the Mao regime it did recognize the integrity of mainland China and Formosa. "It was the Korean war," he said, "which caused the United States to adopt an incorrect attitude on Formosa. And, as is well known, it was the Russians who started the Korean war."

A foreign diplomat with great experience in China returned from Peking after the Ussuri River incidents in the spring of 1969 with this judgment: "It is possible to see how China's relations with the United States might improve. Really, all that is needed there is some American move with respect to Taiwan. But so far as Russia is concerned there is no chance that they will get better. The only prospect is that they will worsen."

What this means, in essence, is that no insuperable barrier exists on the China side to an improvement and normalization of relations with the United States. Nothing in Chinese ideology, philosophy, or national attitudes precludes such a development provided only that, as influential Chinese spokesman have said again and again, the United States will act on Taiwan. If the United States will accept the principle that Taiwan and mainland China are one and indivisible the other differences will fall away. And nothing need change, in practice, in the immediate or foreseeable future. At least so contend the unofficial Chinese Communist protagonists.

But as far as Russia is concerned the case is entirely different. No likely path toward rapprochement, no attitude of reconciliation and understanding can be foreseen. China's case against Russia is so embedded in national consciousness that no resolution through mediation, negotiation, arbitration, or diplomacy can readily be imagined. It has reached the classic point where statesmen turn to "other means."

CHAPTER IV

The River of
the Black Dragon

The Chinese call the Amur the River of the Black Dragon. Three years ago I flew above the enormous waterway during violent thunderstorms which compelled my Soviet passenger plane to bypass Khabarovsk and head straight for Vladivostok (a forbidden city, barred to all foreigners). I could almost feel the aura and mystery which emanates from the great river. It is an enormous body of water, sometimes broad as an inland sea, sometimes spreading across the taiga like a dozen silver fingers. That day the great thunderheads looked like black dragons high in the sky and dragon lightning flashed from cloud to cloud as the TU-104 plunged through the high banks. For a thousand miles the plane followed the River of the Black Dragon, Russia to one side, China to the other. Over China the clouds were thin, white, light—and there was no lightning. The TU-104 pilot doggedly plunged ahead through the menacing storm. The lightning crackled; thunderclaps exploded; violent downdrafts tossed the plane like an eggshell in the surf—but the pilot did not deviate. The dangers of the storm were real, but not as great as the perils of flying over the Black Dragon and the risk of Chinese anti-aircraft guns and fighter patrols.

The River of the Black Dragon is hardly known in the West. Ask Americans to locate the Amur and the percentage who can place it on the Asian continent is slim. The number who could trace it as the principal northeastern waterway of the Asian continent, one of the great river systems of the world, the heart of conflict and controversy between Russia and China for 300 years, would be infinitesimal.

The Amur belongs to the family of Asian rivers—among the greatest rivers in the world but little known outside the Eurasian heartland—the Ob, the Irtysh, the Yenisei, the Lena, the Aldan, the Kolyma, the Amur, the Sungari, the Ussuri. They are north-flowing, and find their way through thousands of miles of forests and tundra to the icebound Arctic and seas tributary to it.

The Amur has its origin in one of the great mountain ranges that form a prickly spine for the Asian heartland—the Yablonovy Mountains, which like the neighboring Altai and Stanovoi ranges are among the world's highest and most forbidding although they are little known in the western hemisphere.

The principal sources of the Amur are two lesser rivers—the Argun, rising in eastern Mongolia, and the Shilka, which springs from the southeastern slopes of the Yablonovy Mountains, east and south of Lake Baikal. The Argun flows northeast and the Shilka more east than north. The two rivers, the Argun running along the northwest Manchurian border and the Shilka entirely within the Soviet territory, join west of Albasin to form the Amur. The Amur for most of its eastward course forms the frontier between Russia and China. At Khabarovsk the Amur is joined by the Ussuri, which rises in the mountains between Harbin and Vladivostok. The Ussuri flows due north, providing the frontier between Manchuria and the Soviet Maritime provinces. At Khabarovsk the Amur makes a left-angle turn and courses north, entering the Sea of Okhotsk at Nikolayevsk.

The menace of the Black Dragon is not new. Conflict between the Russians and the Chinese over the Amur dates back to 1650, the year the adventurer Yerofei Khabarov reached the Amur and the "land of Daurien" after a difficult trip from Yakutsk far north on the Lena, where the Russians had been established for about twenty years.

Khabarov started for the Amur in March 1649, having only a vague notion of what he might find. He was attracted by rumors that in the "land of Daurien" grain was grown, that it was a fertile and luxurious country far different from the subarctic tundra of Yakutsk. He reached the Amur, set up a small fort, and returned to Yakutsk in May 1650 with confirmation of the rumors of grain cultivation. The River of the Black Dragon, it seemed, was under the control of a powerful prince whose capital lay far to the east. The fact was, although Khabarov and the Russians were not aware of it, that the "land of Daurien" belonged to the Manchu dynasty, which had just come into power in Peking. The venturesome Russian trader from the subarctic had unknowingly collided with the outposts of a new, vigorous Peking empire.

Khabarov returned to the Amur in the summer of 1650 with a larger expedition. He captured the capital of a small prince, a village called Albasin, and made it his headquarters, scattering the "Dauriens" wherever he encountered them. Reporting on his initial campaign, Khabarov said that he killed 661 Dauriens, took 243 women and girls and 118 children prisoner, and seized 237 horses and 113 head of cattle.

Peking sent a detachment of Manchu troops to oust the invaders, and the first major battle between Russian and Chinese forces occurred on the Amur near the present-day site of Khabarovsk. The Manchus were defeated with heavy losses. Ten of Khabarov's men were killed and seventy-eight wounded. Three hundred years later fighting was still breaking out on the Amur.

The Russians had opened the River of the Black Dragon and conquered a rich new province. They pushed on and by 1655 had reached the Ussuri. The land of "Daurien" was incorporated into the Czar's empire. The next year an *ostrog*—a primitive fort made of pointed logs with wooden towers and slits for firing, much like the stockades of the American West—was built by the Russians near the confluence of the Nercha and Shilka rivers, 200 miles west of the point where the Shilka joined the Argun to form the Amur. This became the headquarters of the new Daurien administration. At first it was called Nelyudskoi, which means "without people," but soon, with the arrival of soldiers and traders, it became Nerchinsk—a name destined to go down in history books.

For thirty years fighting went on along the Amur. The Chinese would capture a Russian *ostrog*, burn it and slaughter its occupants, and take a few prisoners to Peking to be exhibited. Then the Russians would muster another frontier force and penetrate the lands of the Black Dragon anew.

By this time both sides—distant Moscow and not so distant Peking—had become aware that a major collision was occurring along the remote fringe of their vast kingdoms. The Russians had vainly attempted to establish diplomatic contact with Peking in 1618–19, when their first mission, headed by Ivan Petlin, made its way to the Chinese capital. Petlin did not succeed in winning a reception by the Chinese Emperor but he brought back with him a communication from the Imperial throne which was not translated for fifty-six years; there was no one in Moscow who could read Chinese.

A second Russian diplomatic mission set forth for Peking simultaneously with the first troubles on the Amur, headed by Fyodor I. Baikov. He started for Peking from Tobolsk June 24, 1654, and did not get there until March 3, 1656. After nearly two years of fruitless efforts to conduct meaningful negotiations and numerous quarrels over the exchange of gifts, Baikov refused to make the "kowtow," or gesture of obeisance to the Chinese Emperor. He returned to Moscow in August 1658.

The missions of Petlin and Baikov set a pattern of diplomatic contact between Russia and China—endless dispute, ceremonial disagreements, ultimate inability to resolve the questions at issue. It has continued to the present day.

The attempts at diplomacy did nothing to reduce tensions on the Amur. The Chinese were much closer to the Black Dragon than were the Russians. To Moscow the Amur was like the mountains of the moon—it was so distant, difficult to defend, difficult to keep in mind.

By the 1680's the Russians were hard-pressed. The Siberian traders and adventurers kept moving down to the Amur, but the Chinese attacked and destroyed their encampments. In 1685 Moscow decided to attempt to make an agreement with Peking which would regularize conditions on the frontier, end the fighting, and open up trade with China.

A mission headed by Fyodor Golovin, a very able official, was dispatched to Siberia. He moved east slowly, assembling forces as he went. He had a personal escort of about 500 *streltsi*, crack Moscow guards, and an additional force of almost 1,500 Cossacks whom he recruited in Siberia.

By the time Golovin reached eastern Siberia the situation had taken a bad turn. The Chinese had moved a full army onto the Amur, and had captured the Russian outpost of Albasin, Moscow's only fortress on the Amur. Moscow advised Golovin that he could relinquish Moscow's claim to the Amur as a frontier as far as the mouth of the Seya (at present-day Blagoveshchensk) and that he should abandon Albasin. For practical purposes this meant that the Russians were giving up the Amur to the Chinese.

Golovin's hand was weakened as he progressed eastward. The Chinese steadily reinforced their position. The Mongols south of Lake Baikal rose and almost cut Golovin off from the

rear. The Chinese Embassy, headed by Prince Songgotu, reinforced with 15,000 troops and fifty cannon, advanced west of the
Amur and appeared outside the wooden fortifications of Nerchinsk, a hundred miles east of present-day Chita. Nerchinsk was
far west of the Amur basin.

The game was up for the Russians. Golovin, dressed in a
Russian embroidered caftan lined with black sable, sat down in
a big tent opposite Prince Songgotu, who was dressed in cloth of
gold trimmed with otter and beaver. Golovin did his best. He
proposed that the Amur be the frontier, with Russia taking the
north and west banks and China the south and east banks.
Songgotu suggested that the frontier be drawn at Lake Baikal.

There was a little dickering. Then the Chinese moved their
15,000 troops across the Shilka and surrounded Golovin. Golovin
had no choice. He signed a treaty August 27, 1689. The boundary
was to be the Gorbiza, a tributary of the Shilka, then the Argun
River, and finally the crest of the Stanovoi Mountains, which rim
the northeast coast of Siberia (but which neither the Russians
nor the Chinese really knew much about).

That was it. The River of the Black Dragon went back,
secure and complete, to the Chinese Empire. For practical purposes, major border conflict between Russia and China ceased
for 150 years. The Russian drive to the east was deflected from
its natural goal along the broad Amur. Henceforth the Russians
launched their expeditions far to the north. They pressed forward from Yakutsk, east across the Stanovoi range to Okhotsk
and the icy Okhotsk Sea. They crossed the Bering Straits to the
Aleutians, to Alaska, and ultimately to California. But the frontier
with China remained peaceful and quiet. The question of trade
was settled by the Treaty of Kyakhta, ratified on June 14, 1728.
It set up two places for exchange of goods with China—Nerchinsk and Kyakhta. Boundary posts were set out by the Chinese
across the trans-Baikal and Mongolian regions. Russian policy
followed the lines laid down in 1731 by the statesman Sava Vla-

dislavich, who had warned that "war with China would demand sacrifice of men, time, and money" and inflict damage which would require a hundred years to repair.

Not for 150 years was the River of the Black Dragon to reappear in Russian-Chinese relations, and then it was not because of clashes on the Amur but because of events in China itself—the massive assault on China's isolation and the authority of its empire launched by the British and other European powers in forcibly opening up trade. The opium war put the Amur back on the agenda of urgent Russian questions. When China was forced to yield trade and treaty rights to England the Russian monopoly of the tea trade by the overland caravan routes from Kyakhta was threatened. The whole position of Russia vis-à-vis China shifted.

At this moment a great Russian empire builder appeared on the scene—Nikolai M. Muravyev, who was named by Czar Nicholas I as Governor General of Siberia in 1847. Muravyev had an unshakable conviction that Russia's future lay in the east, in eastern Siberia, in the Pacific littoral, in the lands of the Black Dragon. He expounded his policies in a memorandum to the Czar in 1853. He believed that the destiny of the United States and Russia should be joined—that Russia's sphere lay on the Asian side of the Pacific and America's on the other shore. Russia should look to turning over her American territories to the United States. He told the Czar: "If this takes place peacefully we shall gain other advantages from the Americans. Close relations with the United States are important to us, for it seems natural for Russia, if not to own all Asia, at any rate to control the whole Far Eastern coast."

Muravyev was a man who thought in broad global concepts. All of Asia for Russia, all of North America for the United States. In his thinking and in that of Russians influenced by him lay the genesis of Seward's purchase of Alaska. To Muravyev, China was simply a crumbling obstacle to be brushed aside. And brush

China aside he did. Within little more than a decade of active
exploration Muravyev had planted the Russian flag at the mouth
of the Amur (at that time no one really knew where the mouth
of the river was located), had founded present-day Nikolayevsk
in 1856 at the Amur mouth, and had occupied the coast across
from Sakhalin and set up Russian forts on Sakhalin. He had sent
his expeditions down the full course of the Amur in spite of Chinese protests. He had signed the Treaty of Aigun in 1858, compelling the Chinese to give the north bank of the Amur to Russia,
the south bank as far as the Ussuri to China, and leaving the
question of lands between the Ussuri and the sea for future
resolution. The Russians shared with the Chinese navigation
rights on the Amur, Sungari, and Ussuri. No other powers were
permitted on the waterways. The Chinese negotiators objected
to the terms, as the Russians had at Nerchinsk in 1689, but this
time the Russians had the cannon. The Chinese had none. The
Chinese envoys signed the treaty.

Peking promptly repudiated the Treaty of Aigun, but this
made no difference to Muravyev. He added Amursky to his name,
and henceforth was Count Nikolai Muravyev-Amursky. He
founded Khabarovsk, naming it for his predecessor in empire
building, and in 1860, after hard negotiation, the Chinese were
compelled to sign another treaty with the Russians, the Treaty
of Peking. Not only was the Amur basin given to Russia but all
of the Ussuri area. Muravyev, of course, hadn't bothered to wait.
In 1859, after personally sailing along the coast he picked the
site of Vladivostok, named it, and arranged for the first emigrants
to settle there.

The Far East was now in Russian hands. The Black Dragon
was Russian—not Chinese. This was Muravyev's achievement.

But the story of the carving up of China was not ended.
Russia's appetite was insatiable, whetted by economic opportunity and the competition of the European powers, each trying
to outdo the other in grabbing another Chinese morsel.

In 1896 the Russians got a new treaty from China (in part through bribery—3 million rubles—promised but not entirely paid to Li Hung-Chung, the Chinese Foreign Minister)—a defensive alliance and an agreement to permit the Russians to build the Chinese Eastern Railroad; and in 1898 another treaty was signed, giving Russia Port Arthur, Dairen, the South Manchuria Railroad, and the Kwantung peninsula.

Change came after change—the Russo-Japanese war, the loss of Russian rights to the Japanese, the shattering impact of World War I, the Bolshevik revolution, World War II—but the pattern of Russo-Chinese conflict over the Amur had been fixed.

In each of the diplomatic negotiations between Russia and China there was one consistent theme. The advantage had gone to the side which mustered decisive military force.

How do the present rulers of the Soviet Union, the men whom the Chinese have contemptuously christened "the new czars," view these ancient events? Their contemporary viewpoint, contained in a formal note sent by the Soviet Foreign Ministry to Peking on June 12, 1969, is as follows:

> At the time of the opening up of the Amur region by Russian settlers in the first half of the seventeenth century, Manchuria was a state independent of China and was populated by a people who in ethnic terms were completely different from the Chinese (Han). Moreover, it was precisely in this period that China itself lost its independence and became part of the Manchu state; the Manchus captured Peking (1644) and imposed the rule of the Ching dynasty of the Chinese people. Down to the end of the nineteenth century Manchuria remained a virtually separate formation—a principality that was the direct possession of the emperors and in which Chinese were forbidden to settle or to engage in economic activity.
>
> Late in the seventeenth century the Manchu Emperor Kang-hsi organized a series of military campaigns against the Russian settlers in Albasin province on the Amur. In this connection, the report of the Manchu military commanders to their

emperor noted: "The lands extending several thousand *li* to the northeast that have never before belonged to China have become part of your domains." These Russian lands were held by the Manchu invaders for some time.

In the late seventeenth and early eighteenth centuries the Manchu rulers conquered Mongolia, destroyed the Khanate of the Oirats in Dzungaria, annihilating over a million people—the greater part of its population—and subjugated the Uighur state in eastern Turkestan (Kashgaria).

In this manner a vast area—which to this day is called Sinkiang, meaning "new frontier," and is populated by Uighurs, Kazakhs, Kirgiz, Dungan, and other nationalities—came under the rule of the Ching emperors. At the same time, Manchu-Chinese expansion moved toward the southwest and the south.

This is what reality looks like, if one sticks to the actual facts and does not treat them arbitrarily. China under the Chings was by no means merely the object of a kind of foreign aggression. The Manchu-Chinese emperors, who were a burden to the Chinese people, actively pursued a predatory, colonialist policy, adding to their possessions piece after piece of land taken from other countries and peoples. The process of the formation of China's territory within its present borders was accompanied by the forced assimilation of oppressed nationalities and their physical annihilation. But present-day historiographers in China search through the deeds of the emperors and mandarins only for "arguments" to justify expansionist schemes.

The border between the Soviet Union and China, which came about many generations ago, reflected and continues to reflect the actual settlement of the land by the peoples of these two states along natural mountain and river frontiers. Along its entire length, this border has been given definite and clear legal formulation by treaties, protocols, and maps.

The point at which a clash between great powers moves across the invisible line from possible solution by diplomacy or conciliation and enters the stage at which the military are called in to draft their plans is always difficult to establish.

At what point did World War I become inevitable? Was it when Russia and Austria ordered mobilization in July 1914? Was it when Germany announced her intention of supporting Austria? Did World War II become inevitable when Chamberlain, still somewhat to his surprise, decided to honor his commitment to Poland? Or when Stalin signed his infamous pact with Hitler?

These are questions which cannot be answered positively—the exact little segment in time beyond which there is no turning back; beyond which each crisis may be taken as a causus bellis. Perhaps the Ussuri River crisis is eased over somehow. Perhaps the two sides, meeting in Khabarovsk, are able to agree on navigation conditions on the Amur, Ussuri, Argun, and Sungari for the 1969 season—just as the season is coming to an end. Perhaps the fighting on the Amur does not bring about actual war. Perhaps the outbreak of border skirmishing in Sinkiang passes safely by. But once the ground has been sown with the seeds of conflict each minor crisis, even if resolved, merely makes more certain, sooner or later, the great, the inevitable, the inescapable war.

If the history of collision between Russia and China were of recent vintage; were it the by-product of singular belligerence of Mao Tse-tung and tough-mindedness by the Moscow leadership; if it had an origin in the physical presence of border troops along ill-defined frontiers or of supervigilance of a patrol on one side and hypereagerness of a patrol on the other, then one might say the conflict was a long way from flash point. Neither national interest nor national prestige would be deeply involved. The real Great Power collision must have a long history and it must be the focus of repeated exacerbations in a variety of spheres over a period of years, playing not only on the emotions of the countries but upon the nerves and patience of the national leaders.

It is in such a context that the Russia-China quarrel must be viewed. Its roots, in many ways, go deeper than those of any Great Power rivalry in the modern era. Until the Manchu dynasty began to lose strength in the nineteenth century it was pushing west as Russia pushed east. Over a millennium there had been a constant ebb and flow of power between mobile armies from the East and stable states in the West. In more recent times the peoples of both sides have been confirmed in basic attitudes of hostility and fear, founded on the conflicts of the past and the aggravations of the present; the psychology of "we or they," of surivival or destruction, is prevalent. The middle ways have gradually been eroded until now, on either side, there is increasingly easy and quick reliance upon the military. Negotiation or meeting is merely an excuse for polemics. Neither side has confidence in the other's willingness to compromise or negotiate in good faith.

The military tendency probably is more powerful on the Russian side than the Chinese, and for an obvious reason.

Russia today is stronger than China in every national resource save one—population. Russia has superior national technology, superior national industry, greater organizational capability, more sophisticated defense forces, a larger storehouse of nuclear weapons, superior methods of delivery of nuclear missiles, a bigger air force, a bigger navy, better rockets, better missiles, better artillery, better railroads, better motor transport, more tanks, more armored vehicles, more literate and better-trained manpower.

Russia has these advantages, but each year they diminish relative to China. China may, however (although no one can judge this until combat is joined), possess one immeasurable advantage—superior morale, will-to-fight, and will-to-win.

The argument arises. It has been heard for nearly ten years. It is repeated by Russians to foreigners and to themselves. Better hit them *now* while we have the edge. Better do it before they get the A-bomb (this was the argument in the early 1960's; now it is: better hit them before they get more A-bombs).

The argument is familiar to American ears. We heard it ourselves in the controversy which raged at the end of World War II over "preventive war" against Russia. The argument of those who supported immediate war was simple: Eventually we will have to fight Russia. Let's do it now while we are strong and they are weak, while we have the Bomb and they do not.

The late General Douglas MacArthur put the case in almost those words (as a matter of fact, he made a similar case for attacking China during the Yalu River dispute in the Korean war). The Russian hawks, the members of the General Staff of the Soviet Pentagon, the Marshal Grechkos and others, use the same argument for war with China that our hawks used for Russia a generation ago—eventually, why not now?

One of the "white books" which Moscow has issued in recent months stating the Russian side of the quarrel with China makes 1959 the "definite boundary" in the conflict because in that year the schism passed beyond the point at which it could be resolved by conferences, meetings, third-power arbitration (there have been too many efforts at this by the smaller Communist powers even to enumerate them all) into the realm in which each side now sought not to influence or convince a misguided friend but to impose defeat upon an enemy.

It is almost impossible to fix an exact time and exact year when an international quarrel goes beyond the grounds of the supportable and leaders begin to think of advancing their policy by "other means," as Clausewitz delicately put it. In other words, by force of arms. But perhaps the Russian white book is right. For ten years Russia and China have been living, thinking, planning in terms of the possibility that their quarrel will in the end prove resolvable only by armed force. In ten years habits of thought and conduct are elaborated and take structured form. There is ample time to explore the military possibilities of various strategies, to develop the weapons, train the troops, condition the population, engage in the wearisome and arduous task of trying to line up allies around the world and in the vicinity of the expected conflict. Ten years is not a long time measured in terms of Russian or Chinese history, but amply long to get ready to fight a continental war.

CHAPTER V

Is Mao
a Communist?

During the heyday of the late Senator Joseph McCarthy virtually the entire cadre of American diplomatic specialists on China was destroyed. The McCarthy witch hunt was relentless in the State Department. Almost every American who played any role in China policy in the preceding decade was driven from office, many with their reputations damaged beyond repair.

The charge against the Americans was either that they were "soft" on communism or "soft" in the head. Either, in McCarthy's view, they had conspired to help Mao come to power and to defeat Chiang Kai-shek because they were Communists or "Comsymps" or "pinkos" (or one of the other verbal mudballs of the time), or they were so stupid they did not recognize that Mao was a Communist and mistook him for a mere "agrarian reformer," not perceiving as McCarthy did that they were assisting the Kremlin's "Communist conspiracy" to take over China.

Long since the fatuousness and the vicious anti-Americanism

of the McCarthyite view has been demonstrated by history. The idea of a unified world Communist conspiracy has been shattered on the rock of Sino-Soviet conflict.

But what about the stupid American diplomats who thought that Mao was not so much a Communist as an "agrarian reformer"?

Belatedly and from the most unexpected sources they are finding justification. In the indictment of Mao drawn up by the Kremlin's propagandists very high on the list of charges is the contention that Mao is not, in fact, a Communist but some kind of a "petty bourgeois revolutionary-nationalist" or "agrarian party leader."

Great scorn was heaped, during the McCarthyite period, on those who naïvely accepted Stalin's characterization of Mao. During World War II Stalin often made slighting remarks about Mao Tse-tung. Somewhat to the surprise of his listeners he seemed to value Chiang Kai-shek more highly than Mao, whom he referred to as "a margarine Communist"—a fake Communist. He told Harry L. Hopkins he thought Chiang was more able than Mao and that he didn't think Mao could unite China. Both during World War II and after Stalin turned his back demonstratively on Mao. But after Mao had risen to power, those who, like the late Patrick A. Hurley, had accepted Stalin's view of Mao as a "margarine Communist" were subjected to ridicule. They were, it was said, taken in by the wily Stalin, who actually had been hand in glove with Mao all the time.

There is nothing more difficult to establish than a candid appraisal by one Communist leader of another. Too many factors of ideology, politics, hypocrisy, time, and circumstance enter into the picture. But as far as Stalin and Mao are concerned the evidence is overwhelming that they never were close and long were antagonists.

To try to evaluate Mao and the true relations between the Soviet Communist Party and the Chinese Communist Party requires an arduous, complex journey back into the very beginning of the Communist movement, back to the confused revolutionary days, both in Russia and in China, half a century ago at the end of World War I. Even when we have made the journey we cannot always be certain of our findings. Too much time has passed. Too many changes. Too many reputations lost. Too many men dead.

But some things can be established. In the first years after November 7, 1917, when the Bolshevik revolution was in its heyday, Lenin was much attracted to the China scene, particularly as his hopes for European revolution and specifically revolution in Germany began to dim.

These were years of revolutionary hope and fervor in China as well. The central figure there was Dr. Sun Yat-sen, the remarkable nationalist and democrat, father of China's 1911 revolution, a man who was a liberal to the end of his days but who, in the flush of Russia's revolutionary success and China's problems, was attracted to the Bolshevik experiment.

Lenin had created the Communist International, or Comintern, in 1919 to further the cause of world revolution, and China seemed to be one of the prime prospects. Beginning in 1921 there was increasing contact between Lenin, Russian Foreign Minister Chicherin, his deputy Karakhan, and other high Soviet figures and Dr. Sun and his leading associates. A fledgling Communist Party had been established in China (one of its early members was the thoroughly obscure Indochinese youth known now as Ho Chi Minh). But the chief revolutionary force in China was Dr. Sun Yat-sen and his national revolutionary movement. In this period the Chinese Communist Party, as such, played a minimal role.

In line with the mutual interests of Lenin and Dr. Sun, contacts were established between the Russians and the Chinese although Lenin himself fell ill before any major exchanges took place. The first important Chinese group to come to Russia was headed by the younthful Chiang Kai-shek, one of Dr. Sun's brightest disciples. Chiang and several associates spent three months in Russia in 1923 studying Soviet institutions, particularly the military, as well as the structure of the Communist Party, its Central Committee, and leadership organs, and meeting with leading Soviet personalities. Chiang's visit to Russia made a deep impression on him. Soon thereafter he was to send his son, Chiang Ching-kuo, to Russia to be educated. Young Chiang spent ten years in Russia and married a Russian woman.

In October 1923 Dr. Sun invited to China a group of Russian specialists, most of them military but including some political experts. Dr. Sun's base was Canton, where his government was located. The chief Russian adviser brought to Canton was Mikhail M. Borodin, a veteran Russian revolutionary and member of the Communist Party who had spent many years in the United States, especially in Chicago. Dr. Sun and Borodin had become acquainted in the United States before the Bolshevik revolution.

Borodin and Marshal Blucher (Galin) were to become the chief Russian representatives in China, the intermediaries of the Comintern and, specifically, of Stalin. By the time Borodin left Moscow for Canton, Lenin already was ill and paralyzed, incapable of carrying on communications. Insofar as Borodin received orders he got them from Stalin.

Borodin's task was simple in principle, difficult in execution. He was to help the Chinese carry out a revolution which would bring the Communists to power, presumably after an interim government headed by Dr. Sun. Or, it might develop, Dr. Sun would become a Communist. The question of Dr. Sun quickly became moot because he died, which simplified things. The revolution would be carried out in his name and the name of the Kuomintang, but the Communists would run it and control it.

The general line of tactics Borodin and his associates followed was borrowed from the Russian revolution. The principal revolutionary strength in China was in three or four large cities —Shanghai, Canton, Wuchow, Hankow. Most of the country was controlled by Chinese militarists or foreigners, working together or independently. The idea was to rally the "industrial proletariat" (city workers), form an army, and with the aid of Russian Communist leadership and such support as could be won from the peasants to chase out the warlords and foreigners and come to power. The plan was a by-product of early Bolshevik revolutionary enthusiasm and related in no way to underlying Russian atavistic attitudes toward China and the peoples of the East.

The idea was not bad. It might have succeeded had not Chiang Kai-shek, a brilliant military commander who had learned more than military tactics during his trip to Russia, turned on the Communists and slaughtered them. He did not wish to share power with anyone. The Russians hoped against hope, played out their line with Chiang to the last moment, even encouraged a futile and tragic rising of workers in Canton which produced a fearful slaughter (including the killing of a number of Russians), and then were compelled to decamp.

It was a fateful experience for Stalin. He had hoped a successful Communist revolution would prove his case against Trotsky. It didn't work. He expelled Trotsky from Russia nonetheless, and for practical purposes turned his back from that time on upon revolutionary schemes. If, as seems likely, he preserved to the end of his days a certain respect and grudging admiration for Chiang, it probably derived from his feeling that Chiang was a first-class general, a skilled politician, and a man worthy of his mettle.

There is no indication or sign that the Russians at this time had ever heard of Mao Tse-tung, nor was there any reason why they should have. Mao was a poet, a student of literature and assistant librarian (at eight dollars a month) at Peking University. There he fell under the influence of Li Ta-Chao, librarian and professor of history at Peking University. Mao was twenty-seven years old. As late as the summer of 1920 he had never heard of Marxism. A country boy, a peasant from a middle-peasant family in the province of Hunan, Mao described himself to Edgar Snow as an idealist, a liberal, a believer in democratic reformism and utopian socialism. He had a confused notion of nineteenth-century democracy and old-fashioned liberalism which he hoped to see introduced into China. He was also attracted by anarchism and often talked with his fellow students about the possibility of introducing anarchism to China. The models on whom he based himself as a youngster were the bourgeois liberal politicians Liang Chi-chao and Kang Yu-wei. For a time he was a great admirer of the philosopher-poet Hu Shih (who much later became Chiang Kai-shek's ambassador in Washington).

It was after years of mulling over this odd mixture of political attitudes and theories that Mao moved into the Communist orbit in 1921. He attended the first Communist Party Congress, held in China in July 1921, representing his native Hunan. He had, or so his official biography later contended, formed a workers' circle in Chansha to study Marxist literature.

When the first session of the new Kuomintang was opened by Dr. Sun Yat-sen in Canton in January 1924, Mao's mentor Li Ta-Chao was elected to the Presidium and to three of the principal committees. Mao was one of the 165 delegates. There is no record of his playing any particular role at this time, although his workers' group in Hunan did send a telegram of condolences to Moscow on Lenin's death in January 1924. The nature of the Mao group, however, is somewhat controversial. The Chinese poet Emi Siao, a member of the group who has long been resident in Moscow, describes its discussions as "having an idealistic character, mixing Confucianism with Kant."

Whether or not the description of Mao's study group is accurate, there seems no doubt that Mao's views diverged from the Communist norm. He was expelled from the Central Committee of the Chinese Communist Party in 1924 on charges of association with Hu Han-Min, a reactionary Chinese political leader. Thereafter he was repeatedly subjected to reprimands and reproofs from the Central Committee for his aberrant views. Whether he was ever actually expelled from the Communist Party as some of his enemies have alleged is not completely certain, but one apparently well-founded report states that he was reprimanded on three separate occasions by the Party Central Committee and three times expelled from the Party.

Unquestionably Mao advanced a line which was radically different from that espoused by the Russians headed by Borodin and approved by the Comintern. (Ten years later Mao was to tell Edgar Snow that Borodin and Borodin's advice played a major role in the shattering Communist defeat of 1927.) Mao's contention was that China had reached the stage of "socialist revolution," which in Marxist terms meant that he thought China was a lot farther along the road toward communism than did his colleagues (and Moscow), who took the view that China was only in what they called the "workers-peasant" revolutionary stage. Mao's divergency brought public condemnation of him in 1928 at the sixth Congress of the Chinese Communist Party. The words may seem vague or meaningless to non-Marxist ears; they were not, however, in the heat of the terrible recriminations which followed the utter rout of Stalin, Borodin, and the Communists in 1927. At the Comintern Congress in 1928 Mao's line was attacked in harshest terms, being compared to a similar "error" made by Trotsky in evaluating the 1905 Russian revolution. As the China revolution went down in flames in 1927 Stalin came to equate all criticism of his policies with Trotsky. To link Mao with Trotsky was the ultimate in criticism.

That this made any difference to Mao is dubious. He had not participated in the Communist disasters. He had not been in Shanghai in the spring of 1927 when Chiang Kai-shek butchered Communists by the tens of thousands. He had not been in Canton in the autumn when the ill-starred rising wiped out the remain-

ing Communist cadres. He did not have to flee the country with
Borodin and Blucher—he had already taken to the hinterland.
Far from the industrial cities where the Russians had led the
Communists to disaster, Mao, with small combat units organized
during the fighting in Hunan and Shansi, was forming a base in
distant Tsinganshan. Chu Teh, later to be renowned as the
leader of the Chinese Red Army, and Chou En-lai, foreign minister and premier-to-be, had managed to rally similar small forces
in Nanchang.

Soon they brought their small, poorly armed groups together
and the long years in the wilderness began. It was all wrong from
the Marxist viewpoint, the Moscow view, the Stalin view. Mao
and his cohorts were in the depths of the countryside, not the
city. They were going contrary to the whole Russian experience
(the only valid one, Moscow felt). And, if they succeeded, they
would prove Stalin wrong (probably their worst crime). Mao
was expelled from the Party Politburo and his tactics were dis-
avowed and condemned.

The worst thing about Mao from the didactic, scholastic, argumentative Communist-Marxist viewpoint was his philosophy. In
an article he published in the critical year of 1927 Mao declared
that as soon as possible he would raise "millions of peasants;
they will be violent and as unstoppable as a hurricane. No force
can hold them back. They will destroy all obstacles in their path
and rush on to freedom. They will dig the graves of any and all
imperialists, militarists, bureacurats. . . . They will subject every
revolutionary party and group and every revolutionary to the
strictest examination. Some they will accept. Some they will
reject."

He warned that "the peasant's eyes do not make mistakes."

In evaluating the contributions which would be made to the
revolution, Mao said the peasants would contribute 70 per cent
and city residents and the army 30 per cent. The actual member-
ship of the Chinese Communist Party, as broken down at the

sixth Party Congress in 1928, conformed closely to Mao's mathematics: 11 per cent workers, 76 per cent peasants, 1 per cent soldiers, 7 per cent intelligentsia.

Mao's philosophy, in the view of Moscow, transformed the Chinese Communist party into a peasants' party and Mao into a "peasant-party leader"—the agrarian reformer of the McCarthyite era. Moscow never changed this view. It is still held today.

As far as Moscow was concerned, it is difficult to see that they paid much heed to the Chinese Party after 1927 and their own terrible defeat. Russian interest in China tended to be fixed on the Nationalist government of Chiang Kai-shek (in spite of his earlier massacre of Chinese Communists) or individual Chinese warlords or the Japanese. It was as though Stalin had closed a painful episode in his career. With his increasing preoccupation with the first five-year plans, collectivization of Soviet agriculture, the purges of the 1930's, and the ever-more-dangerous international situation following the rise of Hitler, neither he nor other Russians seemed to have time or interest for the obscure Chinese Communist Party, surviving in the wilderness under the leadership of Mao, Chou En-lai, and Chu Teh.

The polemics between the two countries and the two parties has brought out very little, but what it has produced are bitter and antagonistic charges by the Russians that Mao employed purge and murder to establish his control over the Party in the early 1930's (just as Stalin was doing in Moscow). The victims of Mao's vendettas were—or are now made to seem—friends of Moscow.

It is typical of the long memory and persistence of past controversy that the Soviet charges against Mao go back to 1927 and to the controversial "Autumn Harvest Uprising," his independent military action in Chingkanshan which led Mao into bitter conflict with the leadership of the Chinese Communist Party and caused his expulsion from the Politburo as well as charges that his conduct was "illegal" and contrary to the Party line.

Now, more than forty years later, this hoary dispute is exhumed and made the basis of a Soviet allegation that in December 1927 Mao slaughtered 4,000 of his supporters in the Chingkang Mountains when they sought to break away from his leadership.

He is accused of a series of similar repressions throughout the 1930's and of the execution and arrest of thousands of persons in a succession of incidents both before and after the Communist Party came to power in 1949.

There was one characteristic development. An important secretary of the Chinese Party, a man known as Wang Ming whose real name was Chen Shao-yu, emerged as Moscow's liaison man and eventual representative. Wang became first secretary of the Chinese Party in January 1931 and held the position until Mao replaced him during the Long March of 1935. Wang, still a secretary of the Party, was sent to Moscow as China's representative to the Comintern. There he remained, with occasional trips back to China, for many years. The Comintern was dissolved in 1943 as a wartime gesture to the Western allies, but Wang stayed on in Moscow as Party representative. If he was not originally an agent of Moscow he quickly became Stalin's man, and after Stalin died he did not return to China. He stayed on even though he was a leading member of the Chinese Party, a member of the Central Committee (a post he technically occupied until the new committee was elected at the ninth Party Congress in April 1969).

Wang is now one of Moscow's leading spokesmen in the ceaseless propaganda campaign against Peking. At intervals he recalls unpleasant episodes of forgotten history—maneuvers in the Chinese Communist Party, comrades betrayed or ousted by Mao, skullduggery, intrigue, scandals.

One does not need to take Wang's revelations at face value

to know that there is some basis for the stories. The most important by-product of Wang's exposés is the picture he conveys of hostile distant relations which existed for many years between Moscow and Mao from the time of the Long March in 1935 to the victory of the Chinese Communists in 1949.

If there was any important collaboration between the Chinese Communists and Moscow during the 1930's the record does not show it. Chiang Kai-shek was at the center of Soviet policy. With the emergence of the united-front policy in Europe it was quickly applied to the Far East by Georgi Dimitrov, secretary of the Comintern. The resumption of Japan's attack on China provided a ready excuse in 1937. Everything was subordinated to aid for China—aid to Chiang Kai-shek. Moscow immediately provided military loans to the Nationalists which by 1939 totaled $250 million. They provided tanks, planes (885 in all), armored cars, artillery, anti aircraft guns, ammunition trucks in quantities sufficient to arm twenty-four Chinese divisions. Their aid to Chiang, they like to point out, was ten times that provided by the United States in the late 1930's. They sent some of their finest military specialists, including three men who were to rise to the rank of marshal during World War II—V. I. Chuikov, a future hero of Stalingrad; P. S. Rybalko, a leading armored specialist; and P. F. Zhigarev, a future air marshal. By 1939 they had sent 3,665 "advisers" to Chiang's army and by the summer of that year 400 Soviet airmen were flying for Chiang and some 200 Soviet airmen had been killed in combat. They constructed a military highway from Alma Ata in westernmost Kazakhstan to Lanchow for delivery of supplies (and it also helped them, a bit later, in an abortive attempt to detach Sinkiang province from China).

All this aid went to Chiang and the Nationalist government, not to the Communists. The Communists faithfully followed a policy of a united front with Chiang in spite of the fact that Chiang on a number of occasions used Soviet equipment and

Soviet-armed divisions to attack them. Mao repeatedly asked for aid. None was sent.

Not a few of the military specialists sent to help Chiang in 1937, 1938, and 1939 were the same men who had been compelled to flee for their lives when Chiang turned on the Communists and the Russians in 1927. Now a new and deep comradeship sprang up between the Soviet Union and Chiang, epitomized in a letter Chiang sent to Marshal Voroshilov, then Soviet Commissar of Defense, in June 1939, shortly before the outbreak of World War II, in which he expressed his thanks for the "deep interest and sympathy shown by the army and the people of the Soviet Union in providing China with the material and moral aid which gives her the possibility of carrying on her long liberating war."

There were no such messages to or from Moscow and Mao.

It would have been entirely feasible for Stalin, had he so desired, to channel equal amounts of equipment to the Chinese Communists. He did not do so, nor did he provide aid to them during World War II. His policy was firmly tied to Chiang. It was with Chiang that, on August 14, 1945 (after the Soviet armies already had attacked Japan), he signed a treaty of friendship and mutual aid designed to be the foundation of Russia's postwar relationship with China, a relationship that would continue to be based on Chiang and the Nationalist government, not Mao and his Communists.

Soviet conduct after the defeat of Japan supports the thesis that Stalin expected Chiang would ultimately rule in China. The Soviet forces in Manchuria looted the industries, sending back to Russia or destroying tens of millions of dollars' worth of equipment and machinery, loading up whole plants for shipment back to the homeland. What they left (eventually to be inherited by their Communist comrades) was a shambles. They prepared to evacuate Manchuria in November 1945 but remained until March 1946 at the request of Chiang Kai-shek to thwart an immediate Communist takeover. The Russians held their positions in Port Arthur and Dairen and on the South Manchurian Railroad, as had been previously agreed by the Chiang Kai-shek government.

In the confused and difficult years of 1946 and 1947, when the United States under the aegis of George Marshall was making a vain attempt to persuade the Chinese Nationalists and the Chinese Communists to come to an agreement that would end their fratricidal war and provide for a coalition government, Stalin on at least one and probably more than one occasion strongly urged the Chinese Communists to accept a place in the coalition. He bluntly warned them that Chiang was stronger than they.

If Stalin's policy toward China from the 1927 tragedy onward is examined from the nonideological viewpoint it acquires a distinct logic. It was motivated toward the creation of a viable Chinese state, friendly to Russia, strong enough to provide a certain counterweight to Japan but not strong enough to challenge Russian aspirations as a Pacific power.

Thus, the Soviet objective toward China did not differ too much from the Russian objective in Asian-Pacific policy under the czardom. In both instances Moscow was primarily interested in the enhancement of Russia's position in Asia and on the Pacific littoral. For this purpose China played an essential role. China's existence was necessary to pre-empt the continental field, but neither the czars' ministers nor Stalin had any desire for a strong China.

It is even possible that similar calculations underlay the original Russian alliance with Dr. Sun. It is true that Dr. Sun represented the strongest individual political influence in China and that his movement was truly revolutionary and there was a rational basis for collaboration between Dr. Sun and the Soviet Communists. But had the gambit succeeded and Dr. Sun come to power in a unified China with the support of a strong Communist element, the situation would have been perfect for the kind of manipulation that would have enabled Russia indefinitely to play the role of senior partner to a weaker and dependent China.

Whether or not this was a consideration in Sovet policy from 1923 to 1927, it almost certainly emerged as the dominant factor in the 1930's and 1940's when Moscow based itself on Chiang and his Nationalists rather than Mao and his struggling rural-oriented Communists.

Examination of Soviet conduct in 1945 and 1946 supports this view. Stalin was still playing for the creation of a comparatively weak Nationalist China under Chiang in which the Russian hegemony in Manchuria, North China, and the Pacific littoral could be rebuilt and strengthened and which, while providing a make-weight against Japan and possibly the United States, would afford no real barrier to the consolidation of Russia's long-range Far Eastern dreams.

Stalin—like his czarist predecessors—saw no advantage to Russia in a strong China, even or especially a strong Communist China. There is no evidence that Stalin's successors disagree with him on this point.

Not long before Mao came to power Stalin ruefully told a delegation of Yugoslavs (on one of their last visits to Moscow before the Tito-Stalin split) that he had misjudged the Chinese Communists. He said he had told them after the war that he didn't think they had a chance of winning power in China and advised them to collaborate with Chiang Kai-shek, join a coalition government, and dissolve their government. Mao's representatives, according to Stalin, feigned agreement while in Moscow but went back and took the field against Chiang. The Chinese Communists were right and he was wrong, Stalin conceded.

Stalin kept his ambassador, N. V. Roschin, with Chiang Kai-shek to the bitter end. He was withdrawn from Chiang on October 2, 1949, the day after Mao announced formation of his government in Peking, and sent straight from Chiang to Mao. He stayed until February 1952, when he was replaced by A. S. Panyushkin, one of Moscow's top intelligence men, who had been ambassador to Chiang during the war.

These were the real relationships between Mao and Moscow, between Stalin and Peking, between the warring factions in China, between the Russians and Chiang Kai-shek, between Mao and Chiang. At a minimum they added up to a long history of working at sharp cross-purposes. At a maximum they constituted the record of more than thirty years of exterior collaboration and secret struggle, intrigue and hatred.

This is the record compiled in the years before Mao came to power, before he made his famous trip to Moscow in December 1949, before Stalin died and all that was to follow Stalin's death.

By one of the exigencies of propaganda and the dialectic of the Soviet-Chinese split, Stalin is still a largely discredited figure in Moscow and is sparingly cited in the Soviet polemics. But to the Chinese Communists he has now become a hero. This is a classic reversal of roles.

If Moscow were to open its most secret archives they would demonstrate that Stalin hated, despised, and distrusted Mao from the mid-1920's when Mao, rightly or wrongly, was identified in Stalin's mind with the Trotskyite opposition. On the Chinese side the real record would disclose that there was no one in the Communist movement whom Mao considered a greater enemy, whom he worked more assiduously over the years to thwart and defeat.

It is out of this close-grained, still not completely disclosed record of inter-Party and interpersonal strife that the deepest emotions of the Sino-Soviet conflict were born.

When the Russians add up the record they answer "No" to the question, Is Mao a Communist? As for Mao, he is equally firm. Moscow is not Communist. The Kremlin, in Mao's view, has abandoned Marx for Wall Street. Neither side sees the other as Communist. Therefore there is no ideological barrier to hostility, conflict, war.

CHAPTER VI

The Secret History
of the Korean War

Not many Americans recall President Truman's initial declaration on Communist China and the problem confronting the United States in October 1949 with the establishment of Mao's regime in Peking, the departure of Chiang Kai-shek from the mainland, and the establishment of his government on the island of Formosa in December 1949.

The demand for an American declaration of support for Chiang arose immediately. It was flatly rejected by Mr. Truman. He announced that American power would not be employed in behalf of Chiang Kai-shek, that the regime in Taiwan was a Chinese question, and that the United States was not going to be involved.

What Mr. Truman said in his declaration of January 5, 1950, is worth quoting because it was clear, unequivocal, and has long since been forgotten:

The United States has no predatory designs on Formosa or on any other Chinese territory. The United States has no desire to obtain special rights or privileges or to establish military bases on Formosa at this time. Nor does it have an intention of utilizing its armed forces to interfere in the present situation. The United States Government will not pursue a course which will lead to involvement in the civil conflict in China.

Similarly, the United States Government will not provide military aid or advice to Chinese forces on Formosa. . . .

In case there might be any doubt of the President's meaning, on the same day Secretary of State Acheson said: "The President says we are not going to use our forces in connection with the present situation in Formosa. We are not going to attempt to seize the island. We are not going to get involved militarily in any way on the Island of Formosa. So far as I know, no responsible person in the Government, no military man, has ever believed that we should involve our forces in the island."

President Truman and Mr. Acheson both added that the United States viewed Formosa as an integral part of China.

The British and a number of other European nations immediately recognized Mao. His government was the one in power in Peking and, de facto, the Communists ruled China. What the United States would do was not very clear. Many Americans had remained in China, and although they were not immediately ousted by the Communists they, as well as other foreigners, soon began to be persistently urged to leave. It was not always a matter of urging. Sometimes they were compelled to get out. Sometimes they were arrested.

The American policy, so far as it could be defined at that time, was to "let the dust settle" in China. How long this would take no one was certain. America had been deeply involved, emotionally, politically, militarily. We had poured our prestige into the Marshall effort at reconciliation and when that failed we had tried, belatedly and not entirely wholeheartedly, to lend a hand to Chiang. The whole question of American policy and responsibility for the Communist success had moved strongly into the political arena. The Republicans, sensing a scapegoat, were challenging Mr. Truman and Mr. Acheson. It was a time for political caution. From this Mr. Truman and Mr. Acheson took their cue. They did not rush to recognize Mao, but this did not mean they would not establish diplomatic relations in due course. It was merely a measure of diplomatic and political prudence.

That they had no intention permanently to cut the United States off from China was demonstrated in mid-November, a little more than a month after Mao's regime was established. Mr. Acheson circulated a telegram to a number of American ambassadors, including those with experience in China or holding posts in countries related, in one way or another, to the China situation. He solicited the views of the American diplomats on the recognition question. The replies were quickly forthcoming, and by early December the State Department had in hand the almost unanimous recommendation of the diplomats to go forward with recognition. Mr. Truman and Mr. Acheson conferred, and Mr. Truman agreed that relations should, indeed, be established with Mao. The only question now was one of timing. It was December. Congress was soon returning. It was a difficult Congress. The Democrats had lost control of the House, and the Republicans were pressing very hard. Mr. Acheson favored recognition before the return of Congress in early January, but Mr. Truman decided to put it off until he had managed to get some important legislation through Congress. He knew there would be a partisan row over Mao—better get a little work done before the fighting started. Mr. Acheson agreed to wait for some early opportunity, but the January 5 statement was issued to provide groundwork for recognition when the moment came.

Then Congress met. The partisan scrapping began at once. Mr. Truman had his hands full. In the meantime his Secretary of State made a fateful speech in Washington at the National

Press Club on January 12, 1950. It dealt, not unnaturally, with the Pacific and the new situation which had been created by the rise of Mao, the establishment of Chiang on Taiwan, and the vacuum caused by rapid deterioration of imperial French, British, and Dutch power in Asia.

What Mr. Acheson did was to draw a line of American primary defense in the Far East. He defined it carefully. The line ran from Alaska and the Aleutians to Japan to the Ryukyus (Okinawa) and then south to the Philippines. What we would fight for. What we would not fight for. It was not a lightly made-up list. No diplomat would so assume. He would read it with the greatest care. It was so read around the world. There was on the list a notable omission: Korea.

Here is the precise statement Mr. Acheson made:

> What is the situation in regard to the military security of the Pacific area and what is our policy in regard to it? . . .
>
> This defensive perimeter runs along the Aleutians to Japan and then goes to the Ryukyus. We hold important defense positions in the Ryukyu Islands and these we will continue to hold. In the interest of the population of the Ryukyu Islands we will at an appropriate time offer these islands under trusteeship of the United Nations. But they are essential parts of the defensive perimeter of the Pacific and they must and will be held.
>
> The defensive perimeter runs from the Ryukyus to the Philippine Islands. . . .
>
> So far as the military security of other areas in the Pacific is concerned, it must be clear that no person can guarantee these areas against military attack.

Mr. Acheson did not entirely ignore Korea. He mentioned it twice, but in each instance set it apart from the "military perimeter" area. It was in a different category and we had different responsibilities in Korea from those in Japan, the Ryukyus, and the Philippines.

Quite naturally, Mr. Acheson has displayed great sensitivity over the years to the charge that he had triggered the Korean attack by his National Press Club address. When the late General Eisenhower cited the Acheson statement during the 1952 presidential campaign, Mr. Acheson responded that he hadn't meant to exclude Korea except from areas which the United States would defend alone if necessary. In his memoirs, published in 1969, he returns to this point although insisting that "interest in this old canard has long ceased—except, curiously, among college students." He again insists that he had no intention of excluding Korea or any other area of Asia from United States interest in the event of attack. In fact, however, Mr. Acheson's response to Mr. Eisenhower made clear that there was a decided difference in American attitude toward an attack on Korea and one, for example, on the Philippines. (See Acheson, *Present at the Creation*, page 691.)

Until 1949 the United States had maintained a garrison in South Korea. The Russians had maintained one in the North, but on January 1, 1949, turned the area over to the puppet Communist regime they had installed under their own Soviet-trained nominee, Kim Il Sung. The South was in the hands of an American nominee—a rambunctious and self-assertive one. Dr. Syngman Rhee, who had spent his life in exile in the United States, was now back in Seoul and ardently yearned, hoped, and planned to take over all of Korea (as did Kim Il Sung in the North).

It is, perhaps, typical of the careless attitude of the American public toward foreign policy that Mr. Acheson's notable omission of Korea evoked no congressional discussion, no editorial protest, no debate or questions. It simply was not noticed in the United States.

Washington, deeply preoccupied by domestic politics, went on with its wrangles. The country as a whole was paying a minimum of attention to events in the Pacific and in Asia; such attention as was being devoted to foreign affairs was still riveted on Europe and Germany, where the Berlin blockade and the stubborn conflict with the Russians were the central features of the cold war. Most American interest, at the time, was focused on the McCarthy exposés.

Whether further thought was given by Mr. Truman and Mr. Acheson to the question of Korea or diplomatic relations with Communist China in the late winter and spring of 1950 is not known. Probably not very much. The signs did not seem propitious. Mao Tse-tung had gone to Moscow and on February 15, 1950, the signing of a treaty between Communist Russia and Communist China had been announced. It looked, superficially at least, as though the two great Communist nations had formed a common united front against the world, one for all and all for one. This evoked natural demands in the United States that the "containment" policy which had been evolved to meet the postwar threat of Soviet expansionism be extended around the world to Asia and the Pacific to counter the radically expanded Communist threat now embracing the whole of the Eurasian land mass.

Mr. Acheson had an opportunity to set the record straight on Korea. He made a major foreign policy speech before the Commonwealth Club of San Francisco on March 15, 1950, again talking about Asia and the Pacific. But he let the "defensive perimeter" stand. Most of his talk was devoted to economic aid to developing countries. He coupled this with a lecture to Communist China, warning the Chinese against the Russians (some of his warnings about Russian predatory intentions against China read very well nearly two decades later) and admonishing them on their bad manners, which he said were holding up any action on diplomatic relations and trade.

This, then, was the world as it appeared to Washington as the uneasy spring of 1950 wore on. There was trouble around the world, some of it in Korea. Few states were more hostile toward each other than North and South Korea. There was a series of threats, counterthreats, skirmishes along the border, plots, counterplots, incursions by either side. Each side was highly armed, aggressive, and constantly voicing its determination to take over the other. The situation was tense but there was no indication that it was any more tense than it had been a few months earlier. However, John Foster Dulles, sent to the Far East on a special mission by Mr. Acheson, did take the pains to go to Korea after visiting Japan in mid-June. He went up to the 38th parallel to see the situation at first hand and had his picture taken examining the lines with South Korean officers.

On the night of June 25 fighting burst out at the 38th parallel. Within a few hours North Korean troops had penetrated deep into the territory of the South. The American response was immediate. President Truman made plain that the United States would defend South Korea. Instant action was instituted in the United Nations and (in the absence of the Russians, who were boycotting the UN at that point) the United Nations Security Council on June 27 condemned North Korea as aggressors and ordered all members to defend the South. The Korean war was on.

What had happened? Was Stalin deliberately shifting the axis of the Communist threat from Europe to Asia? Had the action been approved during the Mao-Stalin talks which preceded the Sino-Soviet pact of February 14? Was the action a trial of strength by the Chinese Communists, an initial act in an unfolding plan to conquer and dominate all of Asia?

None of the answers seemed clear in June 1950. Not all of them are clear today. But enough evidence has accumulated to indicate that not many things about Korea were what they appeared at the time they occurred.

President Truman made two responses when the attack came. The first was to rush to the defense of South Korea. The second was predicated on the theory that he was confronted by an omnivarious threat from Communist China. He announced an immediate defense blanket for Formosa. He gave Chiang the pledge denied him in October 1949—all-out American support.

He sent in the Seventh Fleet to block the Formosa straits to Communist China and protect Chiang from attack. He rushed military aid to the Philippines and sent (fateful move!) a military mission to assist the beleaguered French in Indochina.

The words Mr. Truman uttered on June 27 completely reversed American policy on Formosa. He said:

> The occupation of Formosa by Communist forces would be a direct threat to the security of the Pacific area and to the United States forces performing their lawful and necessary functions in that area.
>
> Accordingly, I have ordered the Seventh Fleet to prevent any attack on Formosa. As a corollary of this action, I am calling upon the Chinese government on Formosa to cease all air and sea operations against the mainland. The Seventh Fleet will see that this is done. The determination of the future status of Formosa must await the restoration of security in the Pacific, a peace settlement with Japan or consideration by the United Nations.
>
> I have also directed that United States forces in the Philippines be strengthened and that military assistance to the Philippine Government be accelerated.
>
> I have similarly directed acceleration in the furnishing of military assistance to the forces of France and the Associated States in Indochina and the dispatch of a military mission to provide close working relations with those forces.

The President's actions, across the board, were motivated by the presumption that the threat was a Communist Chinese threat, not simply a North Korean blow and certainly not a Soviet blow. Indeed, Mr. Truman sought to divorce the Russians from responsibility in Korea. In his initial note to Moscow he begged the Russians to use their influence with Kim Il Sung, to persuade him to withdraw his forces from the South. This, of course, the Russians politely declined to do. The whole matter was an internal affair in Korea, they insisted. They did not warn the United

States against intervening; they merely declared against any foreign power meddling in Korean affairs.

Today, twenty years after these events, we still cannot be certain of all the motivations of all the parties. But we can be certain that very little that happened in Korea was what it seemed at the time to Mr. Truman and Mr. Acheson.

For example, there is today every reason to believe that China had nothing whatever to do with the Korean affair. She may not even have been advised that the attack was going to occur; at best she may have been informed, and certainly she had no voice in the plan, its execution, or its objectives although, quickly, she was to be intimately entangled in its consequences.

That the North Korean attack was an "internal affair," as Moscow contended, is equally improbable. There is evidence enough in the belligerent and aggressive conduct of North Korea in recent years to suppose that Kim Il Sung was ready at any moment to mount an armed assault on the South, but that he would have done so without prior consultation, advice, and explicit orders from Moscow is unrealistic. Kim was placed in power in Pyongyang by the Russians. He came to Korea with the Red Army, and he had lived in the Soviet Union for years, like the other Communist carpetbaggers placed in power by Stalin at the close of World War II. He was handpicked for the job. His staff was cleared, like all of those of the new Communist states, not only by Stalin but by his police chief, Beria. But this was not all. Stalin left nothing to chance. Kim had a full complement of Soviet advisers. While Soviet armed forces were withdrawn in January 1949 and all power, demonstratively, turned over to Kim, many Russians remained to advise and train the North Koreans and many Soviet secret-police agents remained to make certain of the loyalty of all to Stalin. North Korea was for practical purposes a dependency of Moscow. It had been so created; it so continued. Communist China did not come into formal existence until October 1, 1949. It did not even send an ambassador to North Korea until August 1950, two months after the war broke out.

Nothing seems more certain than that Stalin was the inspirer of the Korean attack and that the orders came from Moscow. It is possible, to be sure, that Mao was told of the move or that he recommended such action. But in the light of the knowledge we now possess concerning the Mao-Stalin relationship, its extreme sensitivity and outright hostility, it seems unlikely that Stalin, secretive as he was, would have outlined his plans to Mao. It also seems unlikely that plans for Korea had been formulated as early as January and February of 1950. What seems more probable, knowing the working habits and attitudes of Stalin, is that the scheme was elaborated *after* Mao's visit and specifically because of the visit—because of the difficult negotiations, the incompatibilities of the two men, and the conflict in their policies and attitudes that were uncovered in the arduous and argumentative talks.

The trigger which touched off Korea may well have been (as his Republican critics so harshly contended) Mr. Acheson's definition of the American defense perimeter in the Pacific and his specific omission of Korea.

The likelihood is that Korea caught Peking as much by surprise as it did Washington. China was not at the stage in the tidying up of her revolution which called for taking on Korea and the risks which might follow. The Chinese were not in intimate touch with the Korean situation. They had no apparatus in Korea; everything was in the hands of the Russians. They had great problems of their own—the extension and consolidation of their regime in China, the conquest and absorption of Tibet (a very major problem), and, beyond that, one which loomed far larger to them, the tackling of Formosa and Chiang, still not protected by any guarantee or any military forces of the United States. Korea could hardly have appealed to the Chinese as a logical or attractive intiative in the spring of 1950.

If these assumptions are accurate (and there will be no way of proving them conclusively until Moscow and Peking open many more of their secret files) Moscow emerges as the prime mover in Korea. But what was Russia's motive? Was it simply that Korea represented a convenient bit of real estate which could be cheaply gathered up without American interference (as indicated by Acheson)?

This is possible, but again, against the background of Stalin's motivations, it does not sound like sufficient incentive. Stalin was not a gambler. He was not reckless. He was a cautious man. He had tested the United States in various quarters of the world in the years from 1945 to 1950 but never without important motivation. He did not play power politics in a random fashion. If he decided upon a move in Korea he made the decision only within the framework of a calculated means to an end.

American reasoning about Korea invariably begins and ends with the United States. It is presumed that the objective had to be the United States—a weakening of the U.S. posture in the Pacific, a lever against Japan (possibly even a first step toward the communizing of Japan), a shift from Europe to the Pacific in order to relieve pressures on the Soviet position in Germany, etc.

But the United States was not Stalin's only problem. China was a very big problem, a problem of quite a different order, a problem about which (unperceived by the United States) he had already displayed great anxiety.

In view of what is now known concerning Stalin's relations with Mao and the relations of the Soviet Communist Party with the Chinese Communist Party, there was good reason for Stalin's concern. Mao had come to power in China not because of Stalin but, in many ways, in spite of Stalin. The years 1948 and 1949 were years in which Stalin was extraordinarily concerned about and suspicious of foreign Communists everywhere. His breach with Tito fed back into his relations with all foreign Communists. This was a time of purge, trial, and execution—Laszlo

Rajk in Hungary, Tracho Kostov in Bulgaria, Gomulka in Poland, the horrible, still largely secret "Leningrad affair," the anti-Semitic campaign, and the execution of Jewish intellectuals in Russia. It was the time in which Stalin purged the handful of survivors of his 1920's experiments with China revolution—Borodin, Anna Louise Strong, and the others.

Probably at no time in his paranoid career (with the possible exception of his last days) was Stalin more suspicious of every relationship, particularly those with Communists. At this moment the man whom he had for years contemptuously referred to as a "margarine Communist," a man whom he had suspected as a Trotskyite twenty years earlier, a man whose philosophy and tactics were anathema to him (they proved he had been wrong!) had come to power in the greatest nation of Asia, the nation with whom Russia had the longest frontier, her closest neighbor. An ally—perhaps. An enemy, more likely.

Stalin did not stand by quietly acquiescing in the rise of so potent a rival, so powerful a contender. That was hardly his way. He had certain cards to play. He had, for example, his strong position in North Korea. He had his strong position in Mongolia, then run as an extension of Stalin's police state by a local satrap whose tactics and terror matched those of Stalin himself, Choibalsan. Stalin had a strong military position in Manchuria. Russia had clung to special facilities there, having negotiated for their continuance with Chiang Kai-shek and then kept them under the Communists—the great bases at Port Arthur and Dairen, the South Manchuria Railroad, which the Russians now operated not only on its main lines but on its branches into North China. Stalin had—thanks to his agreements with Mao in February 1950 —special positions in Sinkiang province (where Russian agents had assiduously been at work since before the end of World War II and where it was hoped a pro-Soviet principality might emerge).

Stalin had another asset. Typically, it was a secret one, carefully hidden and concealed from his Chinese "allies." He had his own man in control of Manchuria. The Russians had pursued a curious course in Manchuria. First, they looted it; then they hung on for a while, helping Chiang take over; finally they withdrew, conveniently leaving arms for the Communists, probably in the hopes that neither side would be able to establish itself firmly, leaving Russia free to tip the balance or to move in to "maintain law and order." When the Communists won power in Manchuria (sometime before conquering all of China) a special regional organization was set up to administer the province. At its head was a man named Kao Kang, a name that is not widely known outside of China. I first heard it in 1956 when, as a subscriber to the Great Soviet Encyclopedia, I got a notice from the editors to slit out page 213 from Volume 10 and paste in a new sheet. The new sheet contained an article and photograph of the Tibetan city of Gyangtse. The page to be slit out and destroyed contained the biography and portrait of Kao Kang.

This stimulated my interest. Only once before had I received such instructions from the encyclopedia editors. This was when I was instructed to cut out a page containing the biography of Lavrenti P. Beria, the executed chief of the secret police, and replace it with an article about the Bering Sea.

It was obvious that only the strongest motivation would have caused the editors to issue such instructions. Examining Kao Kang's history, I quickly understood what was involved. Kao Kang had committed suicide two years earlier, not long after Stalin's death and Beria's execution. He was then denounced by Peking as a traitor who had attempted to set up in Manchuria a separate "kingdom" of his own and detach the province (the richest, most developed, most industrialized) from China. The announcement spoke in scathing tones about his suicide, which was viewed as a deliberate act to save himself from the hangman's noose or the executioner's bullet which he deserved.

The action by the encyclopedia editors in bracketing Beria

and Kao could be coincidence, but there were circumstances which suggested the opposite. When the Northeast China Region was set up early in 1949 under Kao Kang one of his first acts was to go to Moscow to negotiate a series of special agreements with the Russians. These were, in fact, treaties. He acted as an independent plenipotentiary. At the time it was assumed that this was a device by which Soviet aid and trade could be started with the Manchurian segment of the Communist regime before Mao came to full power and while Stalin still maintained diplomatic and trade relations with Chiang. Kao made a number of trips to Moscow, each time conducting himself as a fully autonomous principal. His Northeast China Region survived the proclamation of Mao's power; he was still running it at the time Stalin died and Beria was executed.

There was no public sign that Kao was plotting to detach Manchuria from China, but, in fact, this was the charge leveled against him after Stalin's death. Inevitably the question arose: With whom was Kao Kang plotting? There was only one area in which conspiracy could have been carried forward—Moscow. In other words, Kao Kang seems to have been Stalin's agent; secretly and without Mao's knowledge, Stalin (possibly through Beria, who was Stalin's principal intermediary with his foreign Communist puppets) had placed his own man in command of the most important and critical single area of China. At any moment Stalin could detach Manchuria from China or employ it as a base for Soviet maneuver.

There is no positive method of proving that this was Kao Kang's role and Stalin's intention. But the equivocal position of Kao has been underlined by the treatment which he is now being accorded (with the full development of the Sino-Soviet split) in Soviet documentation. The customary Communist procedure in dealing with a man who has fallen from favor or who has been publicly denounced is simply to remove his name. He becomes an unperson. This was Kao Kang's fate in Russia for more than a

The wide Mongolian steppe.

A Mongolian horseman riding into a dust storm.

The author with Premier Tsedenbal of Mongolia in May 1969.

Mrs. Salisbury garbed against cold and dust on the Mongol steppe.

A Mongol cowboy with a long pole and lasso herding animals on the open steppe.

A Mongolian family lined up outside their yurt.

Soviet and Chinese patrols clash on the frozen Ussuri River.   SOVFOTO

The Amur River at Khabarovsk.

The great Russian Far Eastern harbor of Nakhodka.

A traditional Mongol storyteller surrounded by youngsters listening to his recitation of poetic sagas.

A family inside the yurt with a tea kettle on their stove.

Kara Korum, the ancient Mongol capital on the broad steppe.

The Buddhist temple of Erendi Dzu, erected on the site of Kara Korum.

Panorama of Ulan Bator.

Above: Chinese volunteer workers happily marching in a parade in Ulan Bator in 1959. *Below:* Chinese laborers ten years later dourly doing repair work on a back-country resort hotel.

decade. Now he has returned to history. He is identified as the chief of Manchuria, his trips to Moscow are reported in historic detail. No suggestion of treachery, no indication that Kao Kang was other than the most honorable of men. To thus treat an individual who was as publicly and sensationally excoriated as was Kao Kang is an act of deliberate and calculated policy. It is an insult and outrage to Peking. It supports the idea that Kao Kang, in Moscow's view, was an honest, loyal patriotic Chinese—honest, loyal, and patriotic, of course, to Moscow.

Now, fit the Korean war against this background. The reality was that Stalin and Mao (by Khrushchev's direct testimony) were on the verge of a full split; Stalin had made strategic dispositions which gave him enormous leverage (his military concentrations in Mongolia, bases in Manchuria, allies in North Korea, and his secret ally, Kao Kang).

If, in addition, Stalin could muster the whole of Korea he would place Mao in a nutcracker. All he need do was squeeze and the Communist chief of Peking would be compelled to do his bidding. Or, more likely to one of Stalin's turn of mind, Mao could be replaced by a reliable man prepared to do Moscow's bidding—such a man as Kao Kang, perhaps.

Placed in this setting Korea acquires a logic which it possesses in no other context.

Of course, events did not follow the course Stalin foresaw. The United States intervened. He had not expected that. The United Nations intervened. He had not expected *that* (and it would not have occurred had the Russian delegates not been boycotting the Security Council). Nonetheless, the gamble almost paid off. The North Koreans almost threw the Americans into the sea. But then MacArthur miraculously stabilized the situation, fought his way back north, and by the end of the summer was striking for the Yalu River. During this time the Russians had played a most equivocal role. They had provided arms and ammunition and materials for the North Koreans, but no Russian personnel; no volunteers; no specialists (or so few they hardly counted).

Now the Korean war took another unexpected turn. As the Americans neared the Yalu the Chinese suddenly became energized. They warned that if the United States went to the Yalu they would intervene. MacArthur ignored the warnings (did he privately wish them to intervene so that he himself might carry the war to China?). In due course the Chinese moved in so massively that it became a Sino-American war. But still the Russians stood aside, even though it is true they provided the Chinese with planes and war materials (which some years later the Chinese painfully paid for down to the last ruble).

By the time the war was over the Russians had lost their domination of the Korean government (of course, by now Stalin was dead). The Chinese emerged as the chief protectors and allies of Korea.

And with Stalin's death the Chinese obtained confirmation—if they had not known it earlier—of the secret role of Kao Kang.

To analyze Sino-Soviet relations without evaluating the secret role of Korea is like trying to produce *Hamlet* without Hamlet. Far from Korea representing a collaboration of the two Communist giants against the West it actually represented Stalin's daring power squeeze against his supposed ally. Or perhaps it was not the most daring attempt. A rumor circulated in the Far East during 1949 and 1950 of a plot on Mao's life, an attempt at assassination which was narrowly averted. There was never any public statement about it. No announcement, no revelation of who was behind it or how close it came to success. But there was a rumor about the rumor—that Stalin and the Russians were responsible.

Today the world still does not know the truth of these rumors. It does not know the whole story of Korea. But Moscow does. So does Mao. It cannot be other than a major factor in the cold passion which has come to animate the Sino-Soviet quarrel.

CHAPTER VII

Image and Reality

The year was 1954 and Stalin had been in his grave hardly twelve months when I first traveled to eastern Siberia. All of Sibera had been closed to outsiders for a generation. The massive system of slave-labor camps, the vast prison administration which had run Siberia as a private empire during the Stalin years, had not yet been dismantled. Everywhere I saw the barbed wire, the prisoners, the wooden guard towers, the spotlights, the tommy-gunners on the alert. There was no attempt at concealment because there could be none. Siberia was a prison, nothing more. It was never quite clear to me why these eastern reaches had been opened to a foreign correspondent. They had not been open before Stalin's death and they very quickly began to be closed again. I guessed it was a flamboyant gesture by Stalin's heirs, who themselves had never been to Siberia and probably had only the vaguest notion of the real conditions. I took full advantage of the opportunity. I visited Irkutsk, Kirensk, Yakutsk, Chita,

Khabarovsk, and Birobijan, winding up at Novosibirsk and Barnaul in western Siberia. I traveled via the Trans-Siberian Railroad. Sometimes I was trailed by as many as a score of Soviet police agents. Police commanders put themselves at my service as "guides" to the cities I visited. NKVD privates chauffeured my taxicabs. It was an eerie, frightening experience. I learned at first hand the fullest meaning of the term "police state."

But there was another impression which I brought back from Siberia and the China border. This was that of a Soviet garrison state. All along the Trans-Siberian I was in military territory. Khabarovsk, on the Amur, was the capital of the eastern Siberian police state, headquarters for the enormous manufacturing, mining, and timber enterprises run by the industrial department of the MVD, but it was also a great military city. Almost everyone was in uniform—police uniform or army uniform. Chita was a pure military city. I hardly saw a man not in the army. It was in Chita that I was arrested for taking pictures in a park. I could not understand why until the courteous Red Army colonel into whose custody an equally courteous Red Army captain had escorted me politely explained that I had been photographing a "military objective"—the park, like everything else in Chita, belonged to the Red Army.

I knew that Chita had always been the headquarters of the Red Banner Far Eastern Armies. What astonished me in 1954 was that there had been no reduction in the enormous forces which Russia traditionally had deployed in the Far East. So long as Japan's Kwantung army lay across the Siberian frontier this made good sense. But the year was 1954. Japan had been defeated in 1945; her Kwantung army had been obliterated by the Soviet forces in a two-week campaign. Nine years had passed, and the Chinese Communist regime had been in power since 1949. There seemed no reason for this huge Soviet military establishment. There were no hostile forces within thousands of miles.

The frontier was that of the country which was Russia's closest associate and firmest ally, yet it was guarded as vigilantly as the demarcation line in Berlin. It was an elusive question. I filed it in my mind along with other curious, inexplicable matters.

For instance . . . I had come to Russia in March 1949. Just a few weeks before my arrival Anna Louise Strong, the American woman who had devoted most of her life to Communist causes both in Russia and China, had been arrested in Moscow on charges that she had long been a secret agent of the CIA. She was held for two weeks in the Lubyanka and then deported. She had come to Moscow a few months earlier to visit her daughter, en route, she fondly anticipated, to China, where Mao was rapidly overpowering Chiang Kai-shek. She wanted to be present at the triumph and had paused on the way to Moscow in Belgrade to see Marshal Tito, apparently in the misguided hope that she might help in easing relations between Tito and Stalin, who were then at the height of their feud.

The reasons for Miss Strong's arrest were murky. One thing everyone knew—she was not an agent of the CIA. A more dedicated supporter of Communist causes had never lived. Some Moscow gossips concluded that the Russians were fearful that she might be an intermediary between Tito and Mao. Beyond that there were no guesses.

Only sometime later Miss Strong's arrest was seen to fit into a wider context, and one which related (still obscurely) to China. She was a very old and very close friend of Mikhail Borodin, whom she had met in China when she was a fiery young American radical from Seattle. With the collapse of Russian efforts in China Miss Strong and Borodin came to Moscow and soon were collaborating on an English-language paper in Russia, the *Moscow News.* For years the two worked closely together. Presumably they shared views on China. What they thought of Stalin and his tactics is not on record—except that Miss Strong even after her imprisonment in 1949 was long convinced that it was an error by underlings which Stalin would have corrected had he known about it. So far as Mao was concerned, her admiration was unbounded and never kept secret.

What neither I nor any foreigner knew at the moment of Miss Strong's arrest in February 1949 was that Mikhail Borodin had also been taken into custody. The *Moscow News* was suspended. Almost the whole of Borodin's staff was arrested, many going to prison for long terms. Others were released after months of interrogation, but Borodin was not released. He died in one of the worst of the Stalin camps near Yakutsk in late January 1953, a few weeks before Stalin's death.

Even today no clear answer is available as to why Borodin and Miss Strong were arrested. Two years after Stalin's death *Pravda* publicly acknowledged the falsity of the charges against Miss Strong. No announcement regarding Borodin was ever made, but his name began to reappear in Soviet historical works a few years ago.

The extent of the 1949 purge of Soviet China specialists is still not known, but it was by no means limited to Borodin, Miss Strong, and the staff of the *Moscow News*. The specialized institutes for China studies and the Foreign Office sections devoted to China were also purged. In the case of the scholars, the arrests and executions were so sweeping that academic publication was brought to a complete halt—the catalogue of books and scholarly articles on China affairs published between 1948 and 1953 shows only three entries of any consequence. After Stalin's death the personnel of the institutes and departments had to be almost completely renewed. The toll of the Soviet China purges was even more disastrous than the parallel purge, under McCarthyite auspices, in the United States.

It is obvious that the arrests were related in some fashion to China and to Mao, to a strain of suspicion and hostility by Stalin toward Mao and those who Stalin felt were Mao's supporters.

Another curious circumstance . . . The year 1949 was one of continuous military success for the Chinese Communists. These were the months when one great Chinese city after another was falling to Mao's armies. Headline after headline in the Western press proclaimed Chinese Communist successes, but the victories got little attention in *Pravda*. True, they were reported, but laconically—a six-line communiqué, an eight-line communiqué. No detail, no color. No editorials hailing the China victories. No long commentaries explaining the significance of the China events to the world Communist movement. Just dry details without embellishment or interpretation. In the total secrecy of the Stalin years this was merely a phenomenon which somehow did not fit the pattern, a detail to remember against the day when it might be understood in context.

Another oddity . . . It was apparent in the West that Mao was going to win the civil war very soon. The tide of battle was running only one way. Yet during the months in which Chiang Kai-shek was falling back again and again from one temporary capital to another, at a time when not a few Western ambassadors gave up and abandoned Chiang, the Soviet Ambassador stayed at his side. Not until Mao's formal proclamation of the Chinese Communist regime October 1, 1949, at a moment when Chiang was soon to leave the mainland for Formosa, did Russia withdraw recognition of the Nationalists, pull out her ambassador, and establish relations with Mao.

One might say that this was merely an example of the Russian fetish for protocol: so long as Mao had not formally announced his government there was no need to remove the ambassador from Chiang. The explanation somehow did not quite ring true. Other nations, including the British, did remove their diplomats from the Nationalists in anticipation of Mao's victory.

Another factor . . . Two and a half months after he had proclaimed his regime in Peking, Mao came to Moscow. It was his

first visit, the ceremonial meeting of the two great chiefs of the
Communist world, Mao and Stalin, an epic event in the history
of communism, celebrating Marxist rule of nearly half the world.
Not since the Bolshevik revolution had such an event occurred.

Or so one would have thought.

Russia has an established protocol for all occasions, great
and small. For this greatest of Communist events the ritual
seemed a bit off key. Mao arrived without prior notice. Press
attention on the first days was correct but no more than correct.
Mao went through the ordinary rounds—the meetings with Stalin,
the banquets at the Kremlin, the visit to Lenin's tomb, the gala
for Stalin's seventieth birthday. Then he vanished from the press
for days at a time. One did not know whether he was still in
Moscow. I remember formally inquiring at the Soviet Foreign
Office about Mao's whereabouts. I got no enlightenment. The
Chinese Embassy was equally uncommunicative. Rumors began
to go around. Mao had returned to Peking. The talks had hit a
snag. Mao and Stalin had quarreled. No one knew whether the
reports were true or false, and it was not even possible to establish where Mao was staying or had stayed during his visit.

One evening another strange thing happened. The Chinese
gave a party for Stalin at the Metropole Hotel. In all the years
of all of the diplomats in Moscow nothing like this had occurred.
Stalin never ventured out of the Kremlin or the security of his
villa in the country. Only once during the war had he gone to
dinner at the British Embassy as the guest of Churchill. No one
had heard of his visiting any other place in Moscow for a social
event. But he came to the Metropole. The hotel swarmed with
secret and uniformed police. Never had such a security display
been seen. Of course, not until later did residents in the hotel,
including myself, know for certain what was going on—that
Stalin had come and been greeted by Mao, standing beside the
great fountain in the center of the Metropole dining room where

guests selected their carp for dinner—the same room where Rasputin had held his orgies when he chanced to be in Moscow.

The question diplomats asked themselves was why should the Chinese hold their party in the Metropole? It was not the finest hall in Moscow. It was not even an "official" hotel like the Moskva, where Party people and important visitors stayed. The reception could easily have been held at the Chinese Embassy or the Hall of Columns or the beautiful and secluded Grand Hotel. Instead, the setting was the Metropole, a hostelry which had an aura of espionage, of second-rate Russian agents, of fur buyers and shoddy party girls. It was as though Winston Churchill had visited Washington and invited Franklin D. Roosevelt to a reception at a down-at-the-heels hotel principally patronized by traveling salesmen and call girls. It was a minor riddle around which arose the aroma of some kind of calculated intrigue or slight, either by Mao to Stalin or Stalin to Mao.

Mao's visit went on and on. Never in Soviet history had there been so protracted a diplomatic negotiation. Mao arrived in Russia in mid-December. Not until February 14, 1950, was the Treaty of Alliance signed, and by this time Mao himself had returned to Peking. Inevitably there were reports of difficult bargaining and hard trading.

These were borne out by the text of the treaty. The whole thing was contrary to Communist procedure. Communist negotiators do not haggle in public or even in semipublic. The general scope of an agreement is carefully worked out in advance, and only after the terms are fully prepared does the chief of state— Mao, or whoever may be involved—arrive. He comes merely to place his signature on a document or documents long since drafted by underlings down to the final detail. The visit usually takes not more than a few days, possibly a week if sight-seeing is included.

What to make of treaties and agreements that required two months to negotiate? Obviously there must have been tough talk, disagreement, threats, argument, claims, and counterclaims.

The agreements had some striking features. The Treaty of Alliance was to come into effect with an attack on either country by Japan or by any state allied with Japan—meaning, of course, the United States. But the United States was nowhere specifically mentioned; only Japan was.

The Russians retained their special position in Manchuria and the Kwantung peninsula, the same position they had first established in the 1890's when confronted only with the weak Chinese Empire, the same position they lost to Japan in 1905 and regained with Japan's defeat in 1945. There were minor concessions to China—joint use of Port Arthur, for example, and provisions for reversion of the bases to China with the signing of the Japanese peace treaty or by 1952, whichever came sooner. The economic provisions caused eyebrows to rise. Russia pledged to give China $300 million in aid (the figure was specified in dollars, which also seemed peculiar) but over a five-year period, making a total of only $60 million a year. This sum was to be advanced in interest-bearing loans, to be fully repaid. Compared to the aid the United States was giving even to small Asian countries this was a pittance and the terms were those of a miser. Nor was this all. Joint Russian-Chinese companies were set up for the exploitation of oil and mineral resources in Sinkiang province and elsewhere. In these joint companies the basic resources were provided by China, technical know-how by the Russians, and the Russians got 51 per cent of the stock and full control—not much different from the kind of deals Standard Oil or Shell Petroleum made with weak colonial countries.

It was years later, long after the death of Stalin, when the talkative Nikita Khrushchev let part of the secret out. He said that Stalin had treated Mao like a suppliant. Stalin had acted the role of the great power chauvinist with a dependent client country. His attitude was so domineering, his posture so overbearing that relations between the two countries came to the verge

of a split. Only China and Russia's shared hostility toward the
United States saved the day. Had the United States greeted Mao
diplomatically, established normal relations in the autumn of
1949, and shown that it was ready to deal with Mao on ordinary
terms, he probably would have broken with Stalin then and
there. The consequences to the world would have been beyond
calculation. The Korean war might well have been averted and
the whole course of the cold war changed. Almost certainly no
Vietnam war would have arisen. To be sure, no foreigner in
Moscow in 1949 had a hint of this. Even in 1954, when I traveled out along the Siberian frontier for the first time and saw the
massed forces of the Soviet Far Eastern armies, undiminished in
strength from the days when they faced the Japanese, any clue
to what lay behind their presence escaped me.

Another event in 1954 has never left my mind . . . This was
a scene enacted that summer. Premier Chou En-lai had been in
Geneva negotiating on Indochina. The negotiations had been
concluded successfully (no one then could have foreseen that
Geneva merely set the stage for the American war in Vietnam)
and he was returning through Moscow on his way to Peking.
The new Soviet leadership—Malenkov, Molotov, Kaganovich,
Khrushchev, Bulganin, and the others of that day—gave him a
reception at Spiridonovka House, the diplomatic palace of the
Foreign Office.

The protocol at Spiridonovka called for the guest of honor
to be entertained in an inner room where he was seated with the
ranking members of the Soviet government and the Party. There
were outer connecting rooms for guests of lesser rank. Diplomats
and secondary Soviet dignitaries primly observed protocol and
stayed in the room to which they were assigned by rank. Newspaper correspondents, however, customarily sidled from one room
to the next until they reached the inner sanctum. On this occasion, when I arrived at the door of the honor chamber I found
that Chou was not alone with the Politburo. The ambassadors of

nations which had diplomatic relations with China were also
present—the British, the Swedish, and the Indian, among others.
Chou En-lai was the life of the party. Glass in hand, he was cir-
cling the table in the gayest of moods, proposing toasts with his
Soviet hosts. This was not unusual. But something else was.
Chou En-lai was offering his toasts in English, a language which
not a single member of the Politburo understood or spoke, although it was a tongue common to all of the diplomats present.
Each time Chou offered a toast his remarks had to be translated
into Russian before the Russians could reply. The foreign diplomats (and the snooping correspondents) did not require an
interpretation.

That Chou's hosts were not exactly happy about his conduct
was apparent. He approached Anastas Mikoyan and proposed a
toast in English. Mikoyan, speaking Russian, replied: "Why don't
you speak in Russian, Chou, you know our language perfectly
well."

Chou snapped back in English: "Look here, Mikoyan, it's
time you learned to speak Chinese. Certainly I have learned to
speak Russian."

Chou's remarks were interpreted, and Mikoyan replied in
Russian: "Chinese is a difficult language to learn."

No harder than Russian, Chou responded. "Come down to
our embassy in the morning. We'll be glad to teach you Chinese."

Kaganovich intervened with a rude remark in Russian but
Chou cut him off sharply, saying: "There's no excuse for you
people."

Watching the play of emotions on Chou's face, aware that
his Russian was certainly the equal of his English, I felt that this
was no mischievous prank by a politician whose spirits were running high because of his success at Geneva. I felt an undercurrent
of deep seriousness below Chou's gaiety. With exquisite Chinese
deftness he was insulting the Russians in the presence of the
diplomatic colony of Moscow, paying back the Russians for a

great many things the Chinese had had to swallow in the past. They knew it. He knew it. When he told Mikoyan it was time Mikoyan learned to speak Chinese he meant more than merely learning the language.

It was against the background of these fragments of evidence, each inconclusive on its own, fitting no pattern, violating all establishment thinking, contradictory to all opinion as expressed in Moscow, Peking, or Washington, that I paid my second trip to the Soviet-Chinese border ten years ago, in 1959. In that year, as far as anyone in the West knew, relations between Russia and China were excellent. Nikita Khrushchev had made a personal pilgrimage to Peking, accompanied by Bulganin and Madame Furtseva, in the autumn of 1954. At that time China had been relieved of the last legacies, so far as then known, of Stalin policy. The joint stock companies had been dissolved. No longer was Russia going to treat China like a rather superior colony. Arrangements for the full return to China of Port Arthur and Dairen and the removal of Soviet garrisons were completed. All the remnants of the special Russian position in Manchuria were liquidated. Khrushchev went even further. He promised China another fifteen factories in addition to the 141 Russia had already agreed to build, restore, or re-equip. The two countries were working closely together. In 1955 a new agreement was signed under which the Russians were to build China's first (peaceful) nuclear reactor. The next year Russia and China agreed to build a joint railroad which would link China's remote Sinkiang province with Alma Ata, capital of Soviet Kazakhstan and the important Turk-Sib Railroad. Direct service was to start by 1960 (the railroad has never been completed).

When Khrushchev's famous secret speech attacking Stalin was made in February 1956, China followed along with Mao's policy of relaxation (his famous "Let one hundred flowers bloom; let one hundred opinions contend"). China ostensibly used its influence in Eastern Europe to ease the unsettling effects of de-Stalinization, to hold Czechoslovakia and Poland from breaking with Moscow, and to try (unsuccessfully) to avert the Hungarian revolution.

This was the surface of Russian and Chinese relations—smooth, warm, cooperative. If there were differences of opinion surely they were differences of degree, not differences in overview or ultimate objective. Each was working in its way—and together wherever that was useful—to achieve Communist goals, to bring communism to power throughout the world. Mao himself had come to the great Moscow assembly of eighty Communist powers in November 1957. The only argument which seemed to have arisen was a dispute over who was to head the "Communist camp"—Mao firmly insisted that the Soviet Union must be at the head and Russia, somewhat unaccountably, declined that honor. The significance of this argument was examined in remarkable detail by Soviet specialists and Kremlinologists of every persuasion. No one agreed on its meaning, but no one felt that it held much more than semantic significance. It was obvious that Moscow did not entirely agree with Mao's 1957 thesis that the world balance of power had now shifted so that, as he put it in his poetic Chinese, "The east wind is stronger than the west wind." But none of this seemed to be the stuff of which cataclysmic explosions might be compounded.

There was a lot that neither I nor anyone else knew about Soviet-Chinese relations in 1959. Perhaps that is why an experience I had in Ulan Bator in July 1959 left such an indelible impression. I was invited to the great Government House, across the Tola River from Ulan Bator, for the reception honoring Naadam, the Mongol national holiday. As I came up a broad staircase I was greeted by a young Mongol Foreign Office attaché and introduced to members of the Mongol cabinet and to Premier Tsedenbal, who stood in the receiving line. Then I was ushered into the ceremonial hall. Instantly I noticed that the guests were not mingling. Half stood on one side of the hall, half on the other. Mongol diplomats and officials moved from one side to the other, attempting to create an air of festivity. But half the guests were not speaking to the other half. To one side stood the Chinese, to the other the Russians. I had to make up my mind quickly where to take my place. I chose the Russian side, as I had found in a few days in Mongolia that no Chinese to whom I had been introduced (except the Chinese acupuncturist who offered to give me a free demonstration of the "cure of the thousand needles") would shake hands with me, and I thought I would have a lonely time on the Chinese side. I walked firmly to where the Russians stood. Soon Mongols were offering me drinks, a Russian or two sauntered up and engaged me in polite conversation. I kept my eyes fixed on the spectacle. The Russians and the Chinese were simply not speaking. True, former Foreign Minister Molotov, then serving a kind of official exile as Soviet Ambassador to Mongolia, walked ceremoniously up to his Chinese counterpart, shook hands, exchanged perfunctory compliments, and then retreated to his own side. I noticed that two aides (bodyguards, I knew) stood beside Mr. Molotov as he talked to the Chinese Ambassador. No fraternizing (and no exchange of messages—Molotov's sympathies for what he regarded as Mao's "Stalinism" was well known) was permitted.

So the party went on. The hospitable Mongols outdid themselves to make it seem like a normal reception with everyone on good terms.

Finally a beefy Russian general came over to me. He raised his glass and offered a toast to "Soviet-American friendship," the inevitable preliminary to all reception conversations with Russians. Then he grew more chummy, came closer, threw a great ham of an arm over my shoulder, and said in confidential tones: "Really now, standing here in Mongolia tonight can you think of any reason why we Russians and you Americans should fight? Is there anyone here to whom you feel more close?"

I could not but agree.

With a gesture toward the other side of the room he whispered: "We must stand together—don't you think so?"

There was no doubt in my mind then and there is no doubt today that the Soviet general in 1959 already was contemplating the moment when Russia and China would fight. He wanted the United States with Russia. Not with China.

That conversation of 1959 has been repeated in a variety of forms since then, particularly in the last two or three years, by Russian officials, diplomats, and generals, to Americans, to Europeans of all varities (even Germans), and to Japanese. There can no longer be a shadow of a doubt as to what is in these Russian minds. They see the day of the Russo-Chinese war drawing nearer and nearer and when that day comes they do not wish to stand alone.

CHAPTER VIII

The Tension Deepens

The death of Stalin March 5, 1953, did not, as those privy to the secret tensions and hatred which marked Stalin's relations with Mao Tse-tung might have expected, produce any real improvement between Peking and Moscow.

Stalin's heirs obviously were acutely aware of the strain in relations. Almost the first act of the new Kremlin leadership was to replace the Soviet Ambassador in Peking, Stalin's old intelligence agent, Alexander S. Panyuskin, with V. A. Kuznetzov, a seasoned diplomat and Party man, but they did very little more. They agreed to give China added economic aid but discussion of the painful and urgent questions which most bothered Peking was delayed. The likelihood is that the Soviet leaders were too busy jockeying for power to make major decisions on China. But that China was important, that China could play some role in the political quarrels which followed Stalin's death was demonstrated, symbolically at least, by one curious event. *Pravda* pub-

lished a faked photograph four days after Stalin's death showing
Stalin, Mao, and Georgi Malenkov, then the heir apparent. The
picture was real enough but it had been cropped, cut, and re-
pasted. Originally taken during Mao's 1949 visit to Moscow, it
had shown Stalin, Mao, and a half dozen Soviet leaders. Malenkov's supporters cropped and cut it to make it seem like a
triumvirate—Mao, Stalin, Malenkov. The purpose was obvious. It
sought to place the combined prestige of Mao and Stalin behind
Malenkov's pretentions. It turned out to be a dud, or worse.
Within the week Malenkov had lost his post as Party secretary
although he continued on as premier until February 1955.

What was significant about the event was the implication
that Mao's smile was not without potency in the Kremlin. What
was significant about Malenkov's defeat was that Mao's smile
wasn't enough to save him. What Mao thought of the matter is
not known, but it was hardly likely to increase his respect for the
Moscow leadership.

Not until October 1954, nineteen months after Stalin's death,
were discussions of genuine consequence held between the new
masters of the Kremlin and Peking. On the surface all went well,
but in retrospect the talks between Khrushchev, Bulganin, and
their associates and Mao and Chou En-lai continued the pattern
of inward bitterness which had so long marked Russian-Chinese
relations.

The concessions the Russians made to Mao were important.
They arranged, at long last, to put Port Arthur and Dairen back
into the hands of the Chinese. The 1952 deadline Stalin had
fixed had long since expired (having been extended under the
supposed exigencies of the Korean war). Now the Chinese managed to regain their territory. The obnoxious joint companies
controlled by Moscow were dissolved. But as for frontiers, territorial concessions, restoration to China of the areas long since
incorporated into the Soviet Union, or the status of Mongolia,
the Russians simply refused to talk. The sudden interest Khru-

shchev displayed in recruiting "volunteers" from the Komsomols for eastern Siberia must have struck a discordant note in Peking. In December 1954 Khrushchev called for a million volunteers to fill up the empty spaces. But not even a million was enough— two, three, four million. Even that would not be sufficient, he insisted. The volunteers began to stream eastward (only to start coming back home again by the hundreds of thousands within a year).

But in other contexts there was an effort by the new men of the Kremlin to get relations with China on a better basis. They began to send large numbers of engineers and specialists to China to assist in the installation of the dozens of new plants, dams, water facilities, and factories being built. Thousands of Chinese students and experts were brought into the Soviet Union. Agreements were made to build experimental nuclear facilities for China and to permit her physicists to study in Soviet nuclear institutions, particularly in a new "Jim Crow" facility set up at Dubna especially for scientists of Communist countries. An agreement was made (in 1956) for joint development of the Amur River basin. There was talk of renaming the Amur "the River of Friendship."

Surface appearances suggested that the Khrushchev regime had found a means of getting on much more smoothly with China than Stalin.

But below the surface there was quite another picture. In 1955 China had embarked upon a positive program of developing her influence in Asia. She sponsored the Bandung conference of Asian powers and made plain to the Soviet Union, which did not participate, her view that Russia was not, in fact, an Asian power. This was the first time China had advanced this idea. Its significance was hardly lost on the Kremlin, although public polemics over China's Asia-for-the-Asians policy were not to occur for nearly ten years.

But the Russians took countersteps. They began to organize

Asian friends of their own. Stalin had consistently been hostile to India, and the Great Soviet Encyclopedia described Gandhi as a British tool and Indian independence as a device for maintaining British imperialism under a new guise. Khrushchev & Co. reversed this policy. They actively wooed India, inviting Nehru to Moscow and embarking on a whirlwind tour of Asia which took Khrushchev and Bulganin to India, Burma, and Afghanistan —the first of many such whirlwind expeditions.

What these events of 1955 actually signified was the opening phase of a power struggle between Russia and China for the dominant position in Asia.

The dramatic events of 1956—Khrushchev's anti-Stalin speech, the upheavals in Hungary and Poland, the general disorder in the whole of the Communist world, China's ill-fated "hundred flowers" campaign—left further deep but hidden marks in Sino-Soviet relations. Not enough has been made public about the moves and countermoves of the two powers to evaluate them with complete accuracy, but the impression endured that China somehow sought to use the crisis in Eastern Europe to increase her influence in the Communist bloc. By offering to act as an intermediary between Russia and Poland and Russia and Hungary, China ostensibly extended a "helping hand" to Russia. But in reality, insofar as China's influence was felt in Warsaw and Budapest, she was acquiring a role and a position in Eastern Europe, which Moscow had always jealously guarded as a Soviet preserve.

In their propaganda the Russians now assert that Mao's hostility to Moscow existed as early as the 1949–52 period but "was still kept secret." At that time, the Russians contend, Mao deliberately sought to sow among the Chinese people a lack of confidence in their Soviet ally, although they do not present specific evidence on this point. It may simply reflect what has become evident in other contexts—that is, that there never was any great confidence between Moscow and Peking and that their underlying hostility was increased by the harsh dealings between Stalin and Mao.

After 1953, Moscow now contends, Mao's anti-Russian tendencies markedly strengthened although he concealed them because China badly needed Soviet aid and because Mao and his group were not yet strong enough to impose their will on the Chinese Party.

The Russians maintain that Mao's antagonism to Moscow grew steadily and became more and more evident in relations between the two countries. It was stronger in 1956 and stronger yet, although still behind a curtain of "hypocrisy," in 1957.

The year 1957 may have been the real watershed and the specific occasion may well have been the celebration of the fortieth anniversary of the Bolshevik revolution held in Moscow in November and attended by Mao.

Mao made a notable address on November 18, 1957, in which he presented two theses. The first was the contention that, as he put it: "The east wind is prevailing over the west wind. That is to say, the forces of socialism are overwhelmingly superior to the forces of imperialism."

What led Mao to make this declaration with its implication that the Communist camp was now so powerful militarily that it no longer need fear the West were the great Soviet technological achievements of 1957—the launching of Sputnik in October, which opened the whole modern space era, the testing of new hydrogen weapons, and the launching of the Russian intercontinental ballistic missile in August.

These were dramatic events indeed. They stole an enormous march on American technology, a march which seemed much greater then than it does now, looking back at more than ten years of enormous development in American technology.

Mao's thesis was a bold one. Although the Russians made no direct answer, significantly they did not accept and elaborate upon Mao's theory that the Communist world after forty years of weakness now possessed the armed might to achieve whatever goals it set.

The second thesis of Mao's has become one of the most celebrated facets of Sino-Soviet polemics, one which has been used against him with deadly and devastating effect by Moscow.

Mao discussed the dangers of nuclear war. He said that of the world population of 2.7 billion a third or possibly a half would die in such a holocaust. He said he had debated this question with a "foreign statesman" who believed that all mankind would be annihilated. "I said that if the worst came to the worst and half of mankind died, the other half would remain while imperialism would be razed to the ground and the whole world would become socialist," Mao asserted.

The Russians and some of the others who heard Mao speak insist that he said that China might suffer 300 million casualties but that 300 million (an underestimate: more likely 500 million) would survive. They also insisted that Mao, in effect, was prepared to run the risk of nuclear war, confident that China and communism would survive, and that he implied that a nuclear war which left the Communist world might not, after all, be such a bad thing.

Mao's remarks have been quoted again and again by Russian propaganda, which uses them to show that China is callous toward nuclear war, even with the United States; that China feels she has a special position because her population is so large she can even survive a war costing 300 million Chinese lives; and that China is even able to find a silver lining to such a war because Mao believes communism would survive. The Russian view is that no one would survive a global nuclear war and that nuclear war between Russia and the United States would destroy the world.

Whatever may be the truth as to Mao's specific statement on nuclear warfare, subsequent events demonstrated that the Soviet Union had no sanguine views in this regard. I have been told again and again by Russians of the terrible danger to the world of nuclear war—usually coupled with an appeal to join forces with Russia against China to prevent such a catastrophe. I first heard such talk from Russian sources nearly ten years ago. I have heard it more and more often with each succeeding year.

Mao's oratory was not the only nuclear event in the Sino-Soviet sphere. On October 15, 1957, the Russians secretly signed what the Chinese later were to call "an important agreement with respect to new technology for national defense" under which they would give Peking "a sample atomic bomb and technical detail for it manufacture." The date of the agreement is probably significant—eleven days after the launching of Sputnik and seven weeks after the successful ICBM test, announced on August 27, 1957. It is probable that there were those in Moscow who shared some of Mao's exhilaration over the "east wind"—that is, who were willing to consider bold adventures (not necessarily Chinese) in foreign policy backed by the force of the new Soviet weaponry.

Mao brought his top military aides with him to the November meeting and they held lengthy discussions with the Russians. There have been hints that the Chinese asked and were led to believe they would receive Soviet assistance in the form of missiles and probably know-how—missile technology and manufacturing resources.

These events, plus whatever else may have gone on behind the scenes, set the scene for the crucial and critical event in Russian-Chinese relations, the one which clearly sealed the conviction of each side that there was to be no resolution of their quarrel.

The Chinese, presumably acting on the basis of Mao's assessment of the relative military weight of the Western and Communist worlds and upon the specific anticipation that Russia would now back them with sophisticated weaponry, launched preparation for an attack on the offshore islands of Quemoy and Matsu.

This precipitated the Quemoy-Matsu crisis of the summer of 1958.

But in the crunch the Russians refused to back China's move. Although it was not apparent at the time, thanks to a judicious issuance of press and propaganda statements, the Russians simply said, "*Nyet.*"

Not all the events in the sequence can be reconstructed in detail, but it appears that the Chinese opened their shelling of Quemoy in late August 1958, either without prior consultation with the Russians or in direct opposition to previously expressed Russian views.

Nikita Khrushchev, accompanied by Defense Minister Marshal Rodion Y. Malinovsky, visited Peking from July 31 to August 3, 1958. Almost certainly there was discussion of the proposed Chinese move. It is possible that Khrushchev and Malinovsky told Mao at that time that they were prepared to put missile and nuclear weapons in China only if they were maintained under Soviet command. They may also have told the Chinese that the price for collaboration against Formosa was joint command with Soviet officers at the top. This was suggested by subsequent angry Chinese polemics contending the Russians wanted to station their own military forces in China under their own command.

In any event, the differences over the Quemoy-Matsu operation were not resolved by Khrushchev and Mao. Nevertheless, on August 23, 1958, Chinese batteries opened fire on Quemoy. A major Far Eastern crisis quickly blew up as the United States announced that it would not only defend the offshore islands but that it would, if necessary, defend them with nuclear weapons.

Russian accounts of that event now describe it as Mao's deliberate "provocation of American and Chiang Kai-shek troops in the region of the islands of Quemoy and Matsu." They declare that action was taken in direct violation of the Sino-Soviet alliance of 1950. Article IV of the treaty states: "Both High Contracting Parties will consult with each other in regard to all important international problems affecting the common interests of China and the Soviet Union, being guided by the interests of consolidating peace and universal security."

The question has often been raised in recent years whether the treaty of 1950 should still be considered valid. The terms of the treaty provide that it shall be valid for thirty years from the time of ratification, which occurred on April 11, 1950. It can be denounced a year before expiry; otherwise it is to run another five years. There is no proviso for nullification of the treaty before expiry date. However, the Soviet declaration that the Chinese violated the treaty by their action of 1958 may be designed as grounds for formal denunciation of the pact should Moscow feel inclined toward such action.

This view is strengthened by the fact that the Soviet "white book" on the Sino-Soviet conflict charges that China again deliberately and intentionally violated the treaty by its provocation of India in the attack of September 1959 on the Indian Himalayan frontier. This, the Russians charge, was a calculated Chinese move to wreck the Soviet effort at détente with the United States, then being carried on by Nikita Khrushchev in the United States. The Chinese action came on the eve of Khrushchev's Camp David discussions with President Eisenhower.

Neither Moscow nor Peking has made any official declaration on the current validity of the Sino-Soviet alliance. However, as late as October 1964 Chou En-lai assured a Japanese delegation that China was certain Russia would come to her assistance in event of war and that the Sino-Soviet alliance was "still very much alive."

Nothing has been said since that time to cast specific light on the status of the treaty.

However, Soviet conduct strongly suggests that Moscow no longer regards the obligation as binding. In the past two years the Russians have made a series of attempts to extend the provisions of the Warsaw Pact to cover the Far East. The Soviet intent obviously is to line up the Eastern European states on her side in event of war and to make certain that they will not stand by as neutral observers if Russia and China fight. (They already have Eastern Europe committed to fight if the Soviet Union and the United States come to blows.) Thus far the Warsaw powers have resisted this effort. At the same time the Russians, in January 1966, strengthened their alliance with Mongolia by broadening their rights of stationing military forces in that country. It is under the terms of the January 1966 agreement that the present large Soviet forces have been introduced into Mongolia. In August 1969 Moscow went even further. She polled the Warsaw powers on the question of a pre-emptive strike against China. The objective of the proposals to the Warsaw powers and to Mongolia is the same. All are directed against the Chinese threat.

Their relationship to the validity of the Sino-Soviet pact derives from the obligations which China and Russia assumed under Article III of that treaty, which provides: "Each High Contracting Party undertakes not to conclude any alliance and not to take any part in any coalition directed against the other High Contracting Party."

While the language of treaties is generally broad enough to permit varying interpretations, it is clear that the arrangements with Mongolia and the Warsaw powers are in direct contradiction to Soviet obligations under the treaty with China.

In fact, if not in formality, the actions of Russia and China have nullified their Treaty of Alliance, although each side may prefer to keep it on the books in hope of a change of government or politics which might bring the arrangement back to life.

It would be repetitious to report in extended detail the catalogue of the ensuing decade—the gradual movement of the dispute from concealed but public polemics (beginning with the time of the ninetieth anniversary of Lenin's birth in April 1960) to the vitriolic exchanges in semiprivate Communist assemblages;

the savage Soviet reprisal against the Chinese in 1960–61 when they withdrew virtually all their experts, specialists, engineers, and missions from China, taking with them the blueprints of the projects on which they were working so that a decade later many of the installations still had not been finished; the meetings between Soviet and Chinese delegations in late 1960, 1961, 1962, and 1963, each time supposedly seeking to heal the breach, each time actually widening it with the brutality of their debate.

The Russians began to bring more and more economic pressure on China. They cut their purchases, they lagged on deliveries of promised materials, they failed to provide replacements, they delivered complex machine tools with missing parts (so the equipment could not be used by the Chinese), they declined to provide military aid (much of China's advanced equipment was Soviet and the burden of attempting to build her own arms industry was enormous).

The Chinese retaliated by cutting their purchases from Russia, and began to seek other areas for trade in the world markets. At the same time the Russians insisted that China pay up to the last kopek the heavy charges incurred for aid programs initiated in the early 1950's. They insisted that China pay for all the arms, ammunition, planes, trucks, tanks, and gasoline provided for the Korean war.

By 1962 the quarrel had become public. Both sides were trading invective. Both were attempting to rally allies among the other Communist movements of the world. The Chinese managed to sign up Albania (which had been fearful of Moscow ever since Stalin offered to let Tito have Albania at the end of World War II), and they established strong positions in many of the Asian Communist parties (but lost most of them during the violence of the Cultural Revolution).

As the conflict deepened in its propaganda, economic, ideological, and governmental involvement, tensions began to rise along the Soviet-Chinese frontiers. Security precautions on the

Soviet Siberian frontier were more strict in 1961 than in 1959.
Chinese travelers in 1959 were accorded special treatment, special waiting rooms, VIP clearance from customs. In 1961 they
were subjected to unusual interrogation, painstaking search of
their baggage, and personal investigation. The special facilities
had begun to vanish. There was a notable rise in general security
—more border guards, more obvious anti-aircraft precautions—a
tension which had not been visible in 1954 or 1959.

Nor was this unfounded. There arose a succession of frontier
incidents, at first quite minor but increasingly more serious. A
critical outbreak in 1962 occurred in Sinkiang, where the Chinese
had been intensifying their surveillance and restrictions on Soviet
citizens and the nomadic non-Han minorities, the Uighurs and
Kazakhs. According to the Russians, conditions became so intolerable that more than 60,000 Russians, Uighurs, and Kazakhs,
including many anti-Soviet White Russians, fled over the frontier
into Russia, throwing themselves on Soviet protection. The Chinese contended that the trouble was provoked by the Russians.
There is no way of establishing the truth. The Russians had been
active in Sinkiang for three-quarters of a century, and had made
repeated efforts to establish Russian authority in the area and
detach it from China. There were many Russian residents there
and an underground (or even overground) network of Russian
sympathizers and agents. From 1949 onward the Chinese had
been attempting to establish their dominance firmly in the region.
Their policy in all frontier areas and with all of the minority
peoples had been firm and repressive in an effort to make their
authority secure in regions where they were racially in the
minority. They had carried out a harsh suppressive campaign in
Tibet for this reason, and it is not unlikely that it had its counterpart in Sinkiang.

What was significant about the Sinkiang outbreak was not
whether the trouble was provoked by Soviet agents or by Han
repression, but that relations had come to such a point of hos-

tility that an armed clash (regular Soviet and Chinese border forces were engaged in the incident) by organized military forces could occur.

The Sinkiang outbreak was to be the prototype of similar clashes all along the frontiers but particularly in Sinkiang, on the Mongolia borders, and along the Amur and the Ussuri during ensuing years.

From 1962 on, the Russians contend, Chinese frontier provocations were carried on in a systematic way under direct government orders.

It was 1962 which marked the complete breach between the two countries internationally, with China attacking Russia for provoking the Cuban missile crisis and Moscow supporting India against the renewed Chinese border assault, and in 1962 the Chinese almost certainly attempted a coup against the Russian-oriented Mongolia government. The effort was thwarted and a rigorous purge of the Mongol Communist Party ensued.

It was from this period that the Russians began to contend that the object of Mao Tse-tung's policy actually was to drive them into war with the United States so that China might benefit. They accused him of deliberately seeking to raise international tensions in order to make peace—specifically peace between the United States and Russia—impossible. They quoted Mao as declaring that "the cold war is a very good thing" and claimed he had told a Latin American delegation as early as March 1959: "Who profits by international tension? The United States? England? The world proletariat? In this the problem lies. I think that none of you should be afraid of international tension. I personally like international tension."

By the mid-1960's the conflict had reached the point at which virtually all Chinese, including students, had been withdrawn from Russia. No Soviet personnel remained in China. Embassy staffs had been cut to a minimum. Embassy personnel on either side were virtual prisoners in their big walled compounds. Be-

fore their withdrawal, Chinese students and diplomats had
organized demonstrations in Moscow and had been clubbed to
the ground by mounted Soviet police riding among the mobs of
demonstrators much as the Cossacks had in the days before the
Bolshevik revolution. The Chinese had burst into the Soviet
Embassy in Peking and had beaten and attacked Soviet Embassy
personnel in the streets of Peking.

The conflict of the two powers had taken a most critical
edge in North Vietnam, where the support of both was vital to
Hanoi. Nevertheless, the struggle between Moscow and Peking
proved more important to the protagonists than the cause of
Vietnam. In 1966 and early 1967 Soviet supplies being shipped
by rail to North Vietnam were hijacked by the Chinese as they
moved south from Siberia to Vietnam, compelling Russia to shift
most of her deliveries to sea routes to Haiphong or to deliver the
goods to Vietnamese representatives on Soviet soil who then con-
voyed the supplies under their personal control.

The Chinese sought to persuade Hanoi to take no more aid
from Russia even though they themselves were unable to provide the sophisticated radar, missile defenses, and fighter planes
Hanoi had to have to protect itself against American air attack.

Both Russia and China often seemed more interested in fighting each other than in helping Hanoi fight the United States.
They indulged in polemics in which each accused the other of
refusing to collaborate in a common effort against "American
imperialism." But to those in Hanoi it was apparent that Vietnam
was just one more area in which the Sino-Soviet conflict was
being fought to the limit.

When Hanoi began to move into negotiation with the United
States in 1968 and 1969, the two Communist powers took opposing views of the prospect of peace. The Russians grudgingly
urged Hanoi to explore peace possibilities, contending that it
could not guarantee or increase deliveries of war materials because of tension with China. The Chinese urged Vietnam to

continue the struggle, contending that it was only the opening battle of the world combat of colonial countries against the imperialist powers.

Behind the argument of each country was clearly visible its hostility to the other. Each sought to fashion from its Vietnam policy a weapon against its prime target: Russia, in the case of China; China, in the case of Russia.

Russia seemed to be looking beyond Vietnam to the coming conflict with China. Her chief concern about Vietnam seemed to be an almost superstitious fear that in some fashion China would succeed in embroiling her in combat with the United States. China, in the initial phase, seemed to believe that Vietnam was the opening battle in the "Russian-American" war of encirclement against China. Later on, when this theory proved unsound, she seemed more interested in turning the battleground against her Russian and American enemies than anything else.

Thus, the more than fifteen years following Stalin's death have been marked by no more than superficial efforts at rapprochement between the two countries. There appears to be even less interest or desire on either side for the fundamental realignment of policy and attitude which would be necessary if a genuine relaxation of tensions was to begin. Instead, the conduct of each side has begun to be characterized, more and more, by the kind of reflexive response which occurs between nations conditioned to deep hostility and antagonism.

More and more this has found its reflection in popular psychology. Soviet spokesmen throughout the first decade and a half after World War II habitually spoke of the United States as the most likely opponent in the event of war. In speaking of the danger of war, the country named most often as the likely instigator was Germany or Germany in association with the United States. Beginning in the early 1960's a change in this formula began to be evident. Particularly after the Cuban missile crisis, when a clear and realistic appreciation of the danger of nuclear confrontation with the United States emerged in Moscow, a variation could be noted in the traditional war formula. For the first time the danger in the East began to be mentioned, in veiled form in public, in frank terms in private. China rather than Germany or the United States now appeared in the minds of many Russians to pose the greatest danger.

A parallel shift occurred in the thinking of ordinary Chinese. Well into the mid-1960's, both publicly and in private conversation with Westerners (they seldom talked with Americans), Chinese tended to cite the United States as the chief threat to China's peace. This feeling was accentuated by the Vietnam war, which most Chinese envisaged as basically directed against them, and many saw it as the opening stage of an all-out American assault on China. Even so, beginning in the early 1960's the Chinese made no secret of the harshness and bitterness of their feelings toward the Russians. Their conversation followed the Chinese government line, which still spoke of the United States as the chief danger, but when they talked of Russia and the Russian threat their personal emotions obviously were far more engaged. Angry words and acid expressions marked their reference to Moscow. Harsh words were used in speaking of Washington but there was a feeling of a mere ritual expression.

Beginning sometime in 1966 the balance began to shift among Chinese as well as Russians. A rearrangement of the order of enemies obviously had taken place in Chinese minds, in part perhaps from lessened fear that the Vietnam war would be used as a springboard for American attack and in part because the quarrel with Russia had become so much deeper and more serious. For the first time Russia began to be named as the number-one threat to China. Often in private conversation the Russian threat so preoccupied the Chinese that the United States was hardly mentioned.

Thus on both sides the general public had reached the point of prewar psychology. On either side, war with the other was no

longer considered to be out of the question. It began to provide
the main content of anxiety concerns. The national consciousness
in both China and Russia was now prepared if hostilities came.
No longer would war with China be a surprise to the people of
Moscow. They feared it in many instances, but they were prepared for it. And the same was true on China's side. Russia long
since had ceased to be thought of as a friend or an ally. She was
seen now as the most predatory of enemies.

CHAPTER IX

The Land
and the Need

In 1952 a book called *Chung-kuo chin-tai chien-shin (A Short History of Modern China)* was published in Peking under the editorship of Liu Pei-hua. Designed for the use of students in secondary schools, it was an unremarkable work except for one feature: a map following page 253 headed, "Chinese Territories Taken by Imperialism in the old Democratic Revolutionary Era (1840–1919)." The map depicted China and its environs as they existed in the nineteenth century upon which were superimposed nineteen legends, each designating a region which had been lost to a "European power."

The areas involved were vast. They included Nepal, Sikkim, Bhutan, and Assam on the Indian frontiers; Burma, the Andaman archipelago, Malaya, Thailand, French Indochina, Taiwan and the Pescadores, the Sulu archipelago of the Philippines, the Ryukyus (Okinawa), and Korea.

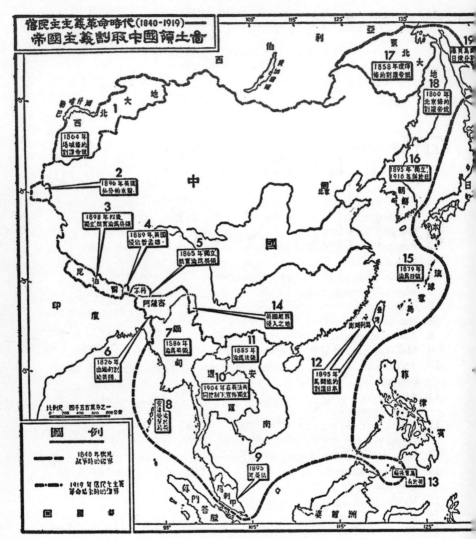

"Chinese Territories Taken by Imperialism in the Old Democratic Revolutionary Era (1840–1919)" from *A Short History of Modern China* (first published in Peking in 1954), a text used in Chinese secondary schools.

KEY TO MAP

(Translation of the information given in boxes on the map.)

1. The Great Northwest: seized by Imperial Russia under the Treaty of Chuguchak, 1864. [Parts of present Soviet Kazakhstan, Kirghizia, and Tadzhikstan.]
2. Pamirs: secretly divided between England and Russia in 1896.
3. Nepal: went to England after "independence" in 1898.
4. Sikkim: occupied by England in 1889.
5. Bhutan: went to England after "independence" in 1865.
6. Assam: given to England by Burma in 1826.
7. Burma: became part of the British Empire in 1886.
8. Andaman Archipelago: went to England.
9. Malaya: occupied by England in 1895.
10. Thailand: declared "independent" under joint Anglo-French control in 1904.
11. Annam: occupied by France in 1885 [covers present North Vietnam, South Vietnam, Laos, and Cambodia.]
12. Taiwan and Peng-hu Archipelago [Pescadores]: relinquished to Japan per the Treaty of Shimonoseki, 1895.
13. Sulu Archipelago: went to England.
14. Region where the British crossed the border and committed aggression.
15. Ryukyu Archipelago: occupied by Japan in 1879.
16. Korea: "independent" in 1895—annexed by Japan in 1910.
17. The Great Northeast: seized by Imperial Russia under the Treaty of Aigun, 1858.
18. The Great Northeast: seized by Imperial Russia under the Treaty of Peking, 1860.
19. Sakhalin: divided between Russian and Japan.

Five other designated regions were portions of China which had been taken by Russia. Two represented a sharing of spoils —the Pamirs, described as "secretly divided between England and Russia," and Sakhalin, divided between Russia and Japan. Three others, one composing portions of Soviet Kazakhstan, Kirghizia, and Tadzhikstan and two in the northeast (along the Amur and the Ussuri, the regions of the Soviet Maritime provinces), were described as "seized by Imperial Russia."

There was one more notable feature of the map. It showed Tibet and Mongolia as fully absorbed into China. There was no mark of delineation to indicate that these regions had any geographical distinction whatever.

The map was also in a second edition of the book in 1954.

It attracted no particular attention until nearly ten years after its first publication, when the question of China's frontiers and her boundary claims began to become of critical interest to her neighbors and particularly to India, Russia, and Outer Mongolia.

The map was then studied for clues to the basic Chinese Communist attitude toward territories which had once formed part of the Chinese Empire. It was noted that the delineations were not essentially different from those which had appeared on maps published under the aegis of the Chinese Nationalist regime. What made the Communist maps significant was the fact that the territorial claims—the concept of a China irredenta— coincided with the actual foreign policy and propaganda line then being taken by Peking.

The Chinese Communist regime has never publicly staked a claim to all the vast areas which once paid tribute in one form or another to the Chinese emperors. In many cases, in fact, Peking has signed treaties regularizing frontiers of countries which the map showed as having once been part of China.

Does the map, then, actually acquire real significance in relation to Chinese policy or is it merely a matter of recorded history—a reminder of the once vast expanse of the empire?

The question can be answered with some accuracy. Maps do possess a definite significance as far as the Chinese are concerned. A number of the areas which are specified as "lost" also appear on the list of boundary regions which the Chinese have declared are still open to negotiation. The most important of these are the frontiers with the Russians. To take another example, *A Concise Geography of China* by Jet Yu-ti, published in an English-language edition by the Foreign Languages Press in Peking in 1964, shows China's borders as being established with all her neighboring states except the Soviet Union. The frontiers between Sinkiang and Soviet Kazakhstan are depicted as "undefined national boundary," as are the frontiers along the Amur and the Ussuri.

The Chinese maps are founded on Chinese state policy. It is no accident that they support frontier claims which Peking has advised Moscow they intend "to settle when the time is ripe."

The total area placed in contention by the Chinese is not inconsiderable.

They have specifically designated territory ceded to Russia under four principal treaties—the Treaty of Aigun of May 28, 1858, by which the Russians acquired territories north of the Amur and west of the Sungari rivers; the Treaty of Peking of November 14, 1860, under which Russia acquired territory east of the Sungari and Ussuri rivers; the Tahcheng protocol to the Treaty of Peking signed October 7, 1864, by which Russia claimed additional territories in western China; and the Treaty of Ili of February 24, 1881, giving Russia territory in Sinkiang province.

The total area is calculated differently by various authorities, but the most recent Peking tabulation asserts that nearly 1.5 million square kilometers is involved. This is broken down as 600,000 square kilometers by the Aigun treaty, 400,000 by the Peking treaty, 440,000 by the Tahcheng protocol, and 70,000 by the Ili treaty.

There is another even larger area which may or may not be claimed by Peking. It is impossible to be precise because the Peking statements are vague and subject to more than one interpretation, but the Chinese appear to be reserving the right to claim 2.6 million square kilometers of additional territory now comprising the Soviet republics of Kazakhstan, Kirghizia, Uzbekistan, and Tadzhikstan. Also unresolved is the status and protection of Outer Mongolia, occupying another 1.44 million kilometers.

In all, this would total about 5.5 million square kilometers. The Soviet and Mongol population now resident in these areas is estimated at above 20 million.

Even these huge claims are not as large as those put on record by the Chinese Nationalists, who list another 656,000 square kilometers acquired by Russia by the Treaty of Nerchinsk.

The question arises as to whether, in fact, Peking can seriously suppose that Russia is likely under any circumstances, short of total military defeat, to turn such vast areas back to China and, if reversion is unlikely except under conditions of military defeat, what lies back of China's claims.

The seriousness surely is there. Speaking with a group of Japanese socialists on August 11, 1964, Mao said: "There are too many places occupied by the Soviet Union. . . . About a hundred years ago, the area to the east of Lake Baikal became Russian territory and since then Vladivostok, Khabarovsk, Kamchatka, and other areas have been Soviet territory. We have not yet presented our account for this list."

And in the spring of 1969 Peking added: "There exists a boundary question between China and the Soviet Union not only because czarist Russia annexed more than 1.5 million square kilometers of Chinese territory by the unequal treaties it imposed on China but also because it crossed in many places the boundary line stipulated by the unequal treaties and further occupied vast expanses of Chinese territory."

One factor has been clearly demonstrated by China in her dealings with other neighbors on territorial questions: she is determined to obtain mutually agreed settlements on a basis of equitable negotiation. The motivation is rectification of ancient wrongs and injustices, the wiping out of past inequalities, and the restoration of national dignity.

But with respect to the claims against Russia another factor seems to be involved. In most cases (except for India) the Chinese have resolved boundaries with their neighbors with a minimum of fuss and no great haggling, but with Russia the Chinese give every evidence of a genuine ambition to recover the actual lands lost to czarist Russia, or at least substantial portions.

At one time the Chinese Communists actually may have cherished some belief that the territories might be given to them by the Russians as a comradely act, on a basis of one for all and all for one, but there has been no logical foundation for such a supposition for many years. No one examining the actual record of the Soviet regime could long cherish the belief that the Russians ever had a real intention of restoring to China the territories taken by the czars.

It is true that Lenin had condemned czarist policy in China, which he called "a criminal policy," and that he had charged the European governments, including Russia, with the deliberate partitioning of China. And in the first flush of revolution Lenin proclaimed for Russia the principle of restoration of lands seized by the czars and national determination by subject peoples. Finland acquired its independence by this means, but Finland was the last example of that policy under the Bolsheviks. Finnish independence was accomplished at a moment when the Communists, clinging to power by the most shaky hands, had few alternatives.

As Soviet power grew, the policy of regathering the lands of the czars steadily made headway. True, Poland and the Baltic states managed to retain independence, but Soviet authority remorselessly made itself felt in the Caucasus, snuffing out separatist movements in Georgia, Armenia, and Azerbaijan. In the Central Asian territories independent regimes briefly flourished, largely under British auspices. They were brought to heel by Red Army troops. The Far Eastern Republic was a creation of expediency as much as anything else, and it was quickly incorporated into the Soviet Union. Mongolia once again found itself a ward of Russia.

The tendency of the Soviet Union, despite early idealism, to move back into the comfortable czarist ruts, territorially speaking, was too apparent to brook any doubt.

As far as China was concerned, Leo Karakhan, Assistant Commissar of Foreign Affairs, in his famous declaration of July 25, 1919, proclaimed that "all secret treaties made before the revolution with China, Japan, or the allies are hereby abrogated" and added: "The Soviet government has renounced the conquests made by the czarist government which deprived China of Manchuria and other areas. . . . The Soviet government abolishes all special privileges and gives up all factories owned by Russian merchants on Chinese soil."

He specifically renounced the Chinese Eastern Railroad, which (by no accident) chanced then to be in the hands of the White Russians, and he renounced Russia's share of the Boxer-rebellion indemnity (also then in the hands of the White Russians). He proposed to enter into conversations with Peking regarding the annulment of the treaty of 1896 (granting Russia special rights in Manchuria), the Peking protocol of 1901 (on the same subject), and all agreements with Japan from 1907 through 1916 relative to China—that is, to return to the Chinese people everything that was taken from them by the czarist government independently or together with the Japanese and the allies.

The Karakhan declaration caused an enormous stir in China. In fact, it had much to do with the close relations which emerged

between Dr. Sun and the Moscow government. It did not, however, lead to any real abrogation of Russian treaties or rights
because there was no Chinese government with the ability or
desire to negotiate with Moscow at that time. Actually, it was a
moment of dire weakness for Moscow. At least part of the motivation of the Karakhan declaration was a desire to frustrate the
deliberations of the Versailles conference with respect to Japan's
claims in the Far East.

At the time of actual negotiations with China in 1924 the
Russians did not, in fact, abrogate any territorial rights. The
question was not discussed. They even hung onto the Chinese
Eastern Railroad, making an agreement to share its operations
with the Chinese. They did, however, formally renounce extra-
territorial privileges and indemnities under the Boxer-rebellion
settlement.

From the time of the Karakhan declaration in 1919 to the
present day—exactly half a century—the Russians have not relinquished to China a single square kilometer of territory taken by
the czars. They have, in fact, made not a few sedulous attempts
to detach more, particularly in Sinkiang.

Thus there was no real basis in 1952, when *A Short History
of Modern China* was published, or in 1954, when Mao raised
the issue with Khrushchev, or in 1962, when Peking began to
make public declarations about return of territory, to believe
that Russia would be in any way amenable to the China demands.

It is reasonable to ask what other factors, in addition to the
consideration of national prestige, might have existed to cause
the Chinese to raise the question of the ancient lands.

China is a nation of 3,768,726 square miles. It is already the
fourth largest nation in the world without the addition of lands
taken by the czars. It is estimated that not more than two-thirds
of China's land is under cultivation, much of it not intensively.
Thus on a basis of statistics China appears to have ample area

available to accommodate a population of almost any size; ample area for the expansion of food production; an extremely favorable overall demographic situation.

The reality, however, is in sharp contradiction to the statistics. While it is true that China comprises vast regions which are sparsely populated these are, for the most part, mountain and desert incapable of supporting substantial settlement. The central areas of China proper have long been excessively populated, but there is a reason for this—they are the fertile and productive regions. Underpopulated Sinkiang, for example, is underpopulated because its vast reaches are hostile to human existence and rainfall is too meager to support agriculture. Examination of arable crop lands in China reveals that her productive areas are already subject to intensive cultivation. The marginal areas available for exploitation (the arid interior regions of Manchuria and Inner Mongolia, for example) have in recent years received large numbers of population, but they have made little contribution to China's food total.

Agricultural production under the Communists has been increased despite a number of setbacks largely attributable to overzealousness in the early days, disruption in traditional agricultural patterns, errors in shifting to larger cultivation units, mismanagement of irrigated areas (with considerable loss of lands due to salinization), as well as weather and climatic factors which continue to play the major role in determining crop yields. Many errors of the early years of Communist rule have been overcome, particularly those which emerged in the drive to establish pure communes throughout the rural areas.

By dint of enormous effort, food production has been maintained in recent years at a level just high enough to prevent (with the aid of large imports of grain) any of the major food shortages, excessive deficiencies, or famines which characterized the old China. But there have been some serious regional shortages and breakdowns in distribution. Nor has there been any

recurrence of the disastrous floods which once made the Yellow
River be called "China's sorrow."

No statistical data has emerged from China since the start
of the Cultural Revolution in 1966, but just prior to 1966 agricultural production was increasing in part because chemical ferti-
lizers were becoming more abundant through the production of
new fertilizer plants. The Cultural Revolution and Red Guard
movement affected rural areas only minimally although rural dis-
turbances in late 1966 and early 1967 caused planting delays.
People's Liberation Army units were sent into the countryside to
help maintain farm production and to assist in spring planting,
summer cultivation, and fall harvests. The result was a bumper
crop in 1967 (excellent weather was the main factor). Production
in 1968 was not as good. Problems appeared in state procurement
and in food distribution in the cities but these stemmed from organizational disruptions due to the Red Guards rather than actual
shortage of food at the source.

Each year for the past half dozen China has imported large
quantities of foodstuffs to supplement her own production so that
she can meet the growing gap between what she can raise herself and what is needed to keep her population from starvation.
In each of the past five years China has spent an average of $500
million or more on food purchases in the international market,
largely grain from Canada, Australia, New Zealand, and, in the
last two or three years, France. Most of the money has gone for
wheat. She has also purchased quantities of rice from Japan and
varying amounts of rice in Southeast Asia. Wheat imports have
ranged from 4.5 million to 5 or 6 million tons a year.

The amount of China's food purchases on the international
market has been roughly equivalent to her foreign exchange
earnings in the Hong Kong trade. China sells to Hong Kong most
of the food which that large international settlement requires—
high-value items such as meat, eggs, butter, milk, fruit, and vege-
tables. She also sells Hong Kong its water, ships 5,000 pigs a day

to the Hong Kong slaughter houses, engages in a considerable entrepot trade based in Hong Kong, and sells textiles and virtually the whole range of consumer goods required by the Chinese population there. The special benefit of this trade to China is that she sells high-value items, receives her pay in hard currency (virtually the only major hard-currency earnings she can depend on), and uses the hard currency for bulk purchase of low-priced foodstuffs such as Canadian and Australian wheat.

The necessity of making up her food deficit through hard-currency purchases in the international market saddles the Chinese economy with an almost intolerable burden. With the Russians and East European Communist countries imposing a tight embargo on shipments to China of machinery, petroleum, armaments, replacement parts, and raw and semifinished materials, the Chinese need every available dollar of foreign exchange to purchase materials for their industrial establishment. Each Hong Kong dollar spent on Canadian wheat adds to the crippling effect of the Communist trade embargo and puts a more difficult burden on the Chinese industrial establishment.

But food must come first.

Even without the Moscow-inspired trade embargo China's food situation would be critical because of the dynamics of her tremendous population.

China's population today is close to a billion. If it has not already reached that figure it probably will in the next two or three years.

This total is so staggering that even in official declarations Peking does not use it. There has been extensive evidence in recent years of a deliberate, calculated effort by the Chinese regime to understate its population. The most recent population figure publicly mentioned by a high government spokesman is 700 million, used by Lin Piao on March 11, 1966. In February 1968 the figure 750 million was used in an official meeting in Lanchow. In reality, according to the estimate of Dr. G. Etzel

Pearcy, geographer of the U.S. State Department, China's population on January 1, 1966, may already have reached the level of 760,300,000 or 800,292,000 or 894,493,000, depending upon which of several growth-rate factors was correct.

If, as many demographers believe, China's population is growing at a rate approximating 20 million per year, it would be, as of January 1, 1970, in a range of 800-million-plus to 950 million, based on the Pearcy projections.

Not the most dramatic aspect of these projections is that fact that the variation between the low-level and high-level figures is almost equal to the *total* population of the United States at the last census.

Moreover, it is apparent that no one—inside of China or out— can be certain within a range of 100 or even 200 million of what the total population actually is.

The problem is complicated by two major factors: first, whether the official Chinese census of 1953 (the only one China has ever had) was accurate or comparatively accurate, and, second, what relationship to accuracy is possessed by the variety of Chinese official statements about population which have been made in the past ten years.

The official census of 1953 gave mainland China a total of 575 million. In 1958 China officially calculated its population (on the basis of registration, not census figures) as 646,530,000. For the next ten years Chinese officials gave the population as 650 million and this was the figure used in all speeches and publications, although in 1964 Mao Tse-tung told Edgar Snow he "thought" China had a population of 680 or 690 million.

A series of provincial population figures which has been abstracted from declarations issued in each Chinese province during the Cultural Revolution at the time provincial Revolutionary Committees were formed does not clarify the issue; rather, it confuses the question even more. If these figures are added up they give a total population of 712 to 713 million, presumably estimated as of 1966–67. Nothing is known as to what the figures are based on. Some demographers believe they may stem from official registration figures of January 1, 1964, and they may, in some fashion, relate to the 700-million population figure advanced by Lin Piao in 1966.

Another series of calculations on China population has been made by John S. Aird of the U.S. Bureau of the Census. He projects a "low" estimate of population of 754 million in 1968 and a "high" estimate of 793 million. In Aird's view, the China census of 1953 was probably an understatement of population and all calculations based on the 1953 figures are likely to incorporate an increasing understatement of China's population.

The key to any projection is, of course, the rate of population increase. Most of Peking's own calculations can be demonstrated to be incorrect because they suggest annual rates of growth radically smaller than those known to be characteristic of China and far smaller than those recorded in similar Asian populations. For example, the 1964 China provincial figures would indicate an average annual growth rate of only 1.4 per cent in the last decade; in some provinces the growth rate is indicated to be less than 1 per cent and in others an actual population decline is reported. Since China has not suffered any widespread epidemics, disastrous floods, great national calamities, or famine the figures simply can't be accurate.

It is true that Chinese authorities have attempted to carry out a rigorous birth-control program. This has been backed with severe penalties against Party members, who have been virtually forbidden to marry before the age of thirty (for men) and twenty-eight (for women). All Chinese have been instructed to have no more than three children, and ration cards for the fourth (and additional) children have been denied. Party members have been compelled to undergo abortions after the second child or risk reprimand or expulsion from the Party. Students have been forbidden to marry, and any children born to them are automatically classified as illegitimate and ration cards refused for them. Paid maternity leaves have been forbidden to mothers after the third child.

Widespread publicity has been given to birth-control techniques in the cities and birth-control devices are sold on street corners and in stores.

But the chief thrust of the campaign, naturally, is in urban centers, and China is still 85 per cent rural. Statistical results of birth-control programs in other Asian countries have demonstrated that there is a direct correlation between urbanization and birth control. No country has had any major success with rural programs because of the basic cultural and economic bias of the peasant toward large families, and that China should prove exceptional in this respect is regarded as unlikely by demographic specialists. They doubt that the Communist campaign has materially affected the rate of population increase. Any infinitesimal decline in the urban birth rate is more than compensated for by the overall decline in death rate as a result of public-health campaigns (the virtual extermination of the common house fly, as one spectacular example), the fall in infant mortality, the elimination of widespread undernourishment and famine, and the absence of catastrophic sources of large-scale casualties.

The general Chinese situation, in the opinion of most demographers, is more likely to produce a radical increase in population such as has followed in so many underdeveloped countries as a result of public health, public sanitation, and other measures producing an increase in life expectancy and an increase in the childbearing portion of the population.

The key figures are birth rate and death rate. In 1963 Premier Chou En-lai gave a figure of thirty births per thousand and said it must be cut to seven per thousand. At that time Western experts believed it was nearer forty per thousand. They doubt that it has dropped much since then. Western specialists postulate a death rate of perhaps sixteen per thousand in 1965. If, as many

believe, the death rate is continuing to drop without an equivalent drop in birth rate, the magnitude of the China population
crisis becomes apparent.

Chinese government figures have suggested a population
growth rate of 2.2 per cent (although occasionally they have used
figures as low as 1.8 or 2 per cent). Western specialists, basing
their calculations on the Chinese figures of 1953 and 1958, note
that during those years—according to China's own figures—there
was a rise of 2.3 per cent per year.

There is no ready exit from this maze of numbers. All they
demonstrate is that the Chinese are confronted with a population
problem of formidable dimensions. That it can be resolved by
national birth-control programs is unrealistic, because even the
propaganda directed to dedicated young Communists is ineffec-
tive in the face of the stronger impulses of human nature. A
Communist visitor to China in early 1969 reported—before any
official declarations—that the Red Guard movement was on
the wane. "It's perfectly obvious," he said, "almost every other
girl in the Red Guards whom I saw was pregnant. Things are
getting back to normal."

Every Asian country is confronted with a population problem of almost insoluble proportions. China is the largest Asian
country. Her problem is even more monumental when juxtaposed
with her food-producing capacity. She can and undoubtedly
will continue to improve crop yields and overall production to-
tals. She can and undoubtedly will continue strenuous efforts to
cut back population increases, but there is no real hope of match-
ing food against hungry mouths with her own resources.

The China population problem was resolved in Imperial
days by natural means—flood, famine, or disease—or war often
intervened to reduce population or to capture new territory to
provide food or living space. Today's Peking rulers will not depend on flood, famine, or disease. But if they cannot feed their
people, if they do not have the foreign exchange to buy the

constantly increasing quantities of wheat and rice, will they sit with folded hands and allow nature to take its course?

The answer, of course, is no. Particularly not when food and food-producing areas lie on their perimeter and when thousands of square miles of those areas once were theirs by right of tribute and subjection.

Behind the territorial claims the Chinese have advanced against Russia lies the harshest logic—the logic of necessity, of life, of existence. The population of Central Asia, of Mongolia, of eastern Siberia is one of the least concentrated in the world (Mongolia, for example, has about a million people living in an area half the size of Europe). The population density of Siberia and Central Asia is comparably small. True, these are not the world's most abundant agricultural lands, but the Maritime provinces of Siberia are a rich natural farming area, hardly touched by the scanty Russian settlers. Mongolia's steppes have been put to the plow at Russian insistence. The experiment is a chancy one, but there are vast regions of Mongolia which could be subjected to intensive livestock exploitation and there are many regions where proper dry farming and irrigation techniques could be employed. The potential of the Central Asian oases has only been lightly touched by the Russians.

China will not starve this year or next for lack of the virgin lands of Siberia. But just over the horizon years of famine can be perceived. Any prudent nation, any prudent national leadership must look to the future, particularly with problems of such scale. In this context Mao's demand in 1954 to discuss with Nikita Khrushchev "rectification of frontiers," as he tactfully put it, emerges as a logical and intelligent exercise of policy. He may well have known that the Russians were not likely to talk about the question or meet his demands, but the harsh exigencies of Chinese reality compelled him to raise the question.

It may seem like a line out of a bad Nazi propaganda picture, but Chinese Lebensraum is no figment of a Chinese Goebbels. It is a basic criterion for the existence of China into the twenty-first century, when—in all probability—her population will number close to 2 billion and when one out of every three human beings on the planet will be Chinese.

Confronted with the dilemma of starve or fight, the Chinese really have no alternative. They will—and must—fight.

CHAPTER X

"To Teach Them a Lesson"

The highway north of Ulan Bator runs in an almost straight line toward the Russian frontier, 250 miles distant. It is a macadam-surfaced road and when I first traveled it ten years ago it petered out five or six miles beyond the city, close enough so that you could still look back and see the high tower of the new flour mill and the grain elevators stark against the flat plain and, dimly in the distance, the tile-and-gilt roof of the Gandjan monastery in the high foothills just behind Ulan Bator.

Now the macadam continues a hundred kilometers north of Ulan Bator and the road would be better if it did not. The highway is simply a tar surface laid on the old horse-and-sheep trail across the open steppe. It ruts, cracks, and heaves in the cold Mongolian winters and the hot Mongolian summers, and what had been a firm, hard-packed steppe turns into a sleazy, pitted road, as rough for jeep and truck travel as any you are likely to encounter. Only when the jeep swings out onto the grass does the jolting halt. In Mongolia nature has built a better highway than man.

There are few towns and few villages in Mongolia. You can travel for miles across the steppe without encountering a cluster of human habitations—only an occasional caravansary, gaunt and isolated on the open plain; a herdsman's encampment of half a dozen white conical yurts set up against the shoulder of a foothill; a new state farm with buildings of whitewashed plaster and log cabins that remind you of Siberia.

The road north from Ulan Bator is no exception to the rule but, as it follows the Trans-Mongolia Railroad, you do encounter railroad settlements and occasional district distribution points with a store or two, a small warehouse, a corral for horses, a few houses, and a district, or *aymak*, office.

An hour or two north of Ulan Bator we came to a new town, a half-finished town, the scene of feverish construction. It was being built beside the railroad. There was a large fenced area for construction supplies—lumber, prestressed concrete, wire, and steel rods—guarded by barbed wire and watchtowers. A petrol dump had been installed and olive-drab army trucks rumbled across the scene. A score of buildings were in various stages of construction. Some barracks up against the foothills, three-story brick buildings, had been finished. Others were going up. It was the busiest scene I had witnessed in Mongolia, but it was not a Mongol town. The red banners across the village street hailing "fulfillment of the plan" by May Day were in Russian. The carpenters whose hammers echoed to the foothills and back were Russian. The slow-moving attendant at the petrol pumps was Russian. The bricklayers were Russian. The truck drivers were Russian.

These were not ordinary Russians hired in Siberia to work in Mongolia at premium pay. These were Red Army troops, construction forces carrying out a rush job. Nor was this a Mongolian village being put up for the use of Mongol collective farmers. This was a Russian military base, a *voenny gorodok,* being rushed to completion. For what purpose? That, obviously, no one was talking about. But looking at the concrete bunkers neatly nestled into the shoulder of a rank of hills facing south, looking at the radar complex installed on a mountain crest where it commanded all approaches, one could guess that this was something more than a simple supply dump or the headquarters of a civilian construction regiment.

The *voenny gorodok* in the hills north of Ulan Bator was not a unique installation, nor was the fevered pace of construction in the late spring of 1969 unusual. The pace was characteristic and the *voenny gorodok* was only one of an unknown number of secret military installations being rushed to completion in Mongolia. The nature of the installations could be guessed by noting the shoulder tabs of the throngs of Soviet officers and men to be seen almost everywhere in Mongolia, which showed that the bulk of the troops were rocket and missile forces, artillery men, airmen, and tank men.

The building of the *voenny gorodok* on the north-south Trans-Mongol Railroad was no accident. The railroad runs south from Irkutsk and Ulan-Ude (capital of Buryatia—formerly Buryat-Mongolia) and forms the core for the Soviet military dispositions in Mongolia. The railroad continues south from Ulan Bator, reaching the Chinese frontier at Dzamyn Ude. The railroad, jointly operated by the Russians and the Mongols, was completed in the broad Russian gauge in 1956. The broad gauge then ran right across Mongolia and sixty miles into China to the city of Tsining, a junction point where the switch to the narrower Chinese gauge was made. But no longer. The Chinese in 1966 tore up the broad Russian lines and laid their own tracks up to Dzamyn Ude. No more Russian or Mongol trains on Chinese territory.

Soviet military dispositions follow the rail line south across the Gobi. No diplomat has traveled extensively in that area, but those who go back and forth from Peking along the railroad have seen enough to be aware that this is a major Soviet concentration area. They have no doubt that missiles have been installed in locations not far from the rail right-of-way in southern Mongolia.

The railroads are the key to Soviet missile deployment. The Mongol steppe is adequate or more than adequate for movement of troops, trucks, and tanks, but for the delicate and elaborate apparatus required for missilery the railroads are essential because of the absence of real roads.

There are no roads in western Mongolia (only tracks across the steppe) and no travelers in that area have seen any indications of important Soviet military interest. The only other railroad line in Mongolia is in the eastern tip of the country, the Mongolian arrowhead which projects into Manchuria across the Khalkin-gol River. Here a branch from the Trans-Siberian breaks off from the old Russian link to the Chinese Eastern Railroad from Chita. It branches just west of Manchouli and cuts down into Mongolia to Choibalsan, the metropolis of eastern Mongolia. Choibalsan is the second or third city of Mongolia. It and Darkhan have nearly equal populations—around 24,000—and they are the only cities of any size in the country in addition to Ulan Bator. The railroad runs through Choibalsan and continues to Tamsag-Bulak, well forward on the tip of the Mongol arrowhead.

Foreign diplomats have not visited Choibalsan for a number of years, not even Eastern European Communists or the several thousand specialists in Mongolia have been permitted in this area. Here, behind the Khalkin-gol, is the second major area of Soviet military concentration.

These are some of the forces the Soviets now have available to carry out Moscow's command when and if the order to "teach them a lesson" is issued. Precisely what meaning should be attached to that expression—so often repeated by Soviet military men in talking about China and privately reiterated by Soviet political figures, and not infrequently by ordinary Russians—cannot be stated.

But the character of Soviet forces deployed into Mongolia and eastern Siberia and the general location of their concentrations provides a clear indication. There are two major dispositions in Mongolia—in the south along the Trans-Mongolian Railroad and in the east near the Khalkin-gol. In Siberia itself the principal concentrations have been observed in the Chita area (the headquarters of the Red Banner Far Eastern Armies), farther east in the Blagoveshchensk and Khabarovsk areas, and in the Maritime provinces along the Ussuri River frontier.

The high percentage of missile and rocket forces, together with very blunt speaking on the part of the Russians concerning the use of "modern weapons," supports the conviction (and fear) of the Chinese that the Russians are prepared to attack with nuclear as well as conventional arms. It is difficult to believe that the missile installations which have been rushed into completion along the Chinese frontiers have not been armed with nuclear warheads. The locations suggest the possibility of a strike against the known Chinese nuclear production and testing facilities at Lanchow, Paotow, and Lop Nor, all of which lie within 200 to 300 miles of the Soviet bases—well within missile range.

Supporting the theory that the Russians are prepared to attack Chinese nuclear capability is a Soviet thesis which has been advanced repeatedly since 1957 (ever since Mao Tse-tung's famous declaration which the Russians interpret as indicating a Chinese willingness to utilize nuclear war in behalf of their revolutionary aspirations). The Russians have said again and again in private conversations in the last decade that the United States and Russia must hasten to arrive at an agreement on nuclear questions *before* the Chinese acquire nuclear weapons because once China has atomic bombs she will use them. The Russian argument might have been simply self-serving, an effort to maintain the U.S.-U.S.S.R. monopoly of nuclear arms so far as possible. But it has continued to be pressed urgently by the Russians even after the Chinese acquired nuclear capability in 1964. The argument is slightly, but only slightly, changed. It is now that U.S.-U.S.S.R. agreement is even more urgent because with nuclear weapons in hand the Chinese may use them at any moment. *Pravda* put the case bluntly and squarely in an editorial of August 29, 1969: if war comes with China *it will be nuclear.* No ifs, ands, or buts.

There is every reason to believe that the Russians have convinced themselves that if war comes China will use her nuclear arms. This being true, Moscow must strike first and destroy China's capability of retaliation. In this argument the Soviet military voices weigh in heavily in favor of a pre-emptive blow against China.

Such a strike would closely fit the pattern of the war the Soviet military are prepared to wage in the Far East. There is no difficulty in constructing an approximation of the Soviet war plan against China, because the outline of past campaigns in the region are so detailed and well known.

Russia has fought two major wars in China in this century, one major campaign, several minor but important border clashes, and, in Mongolia and Siberia, a complicated mixture of guerrilla and civil war. There is no geographical area in which the Russians have had more extensive military experience. In these engagements they suffered one disastrous defeat—that of 1904–5 at the hands of the Japanese. The other encounters have been successful, two of them remarkably so. It is unquestionably on the pattern of the two most successful and most recent Red Army engagements in the Far East that the battle plans for the China war are based.

The Russians learned one major fact from the 1904–5 disaster against Japan: to fight successfully in the Far East you must muster superior forces and maintain them effectively at the end of a 4,000-mile land supply line. The inadequacy of the numbers of czarist troops brought into action against Japan was not as fatal as the inability of the incomplete Trans-Siberian Railroad to supply, reinforce, and provision the Czar's armies in Manchuria. And the task could not be accomplished by sea.

This lesson was fully absorbed by the Bolshevik regime. They won back Siberia (and Mongolia) in painstaking fighting that proceeded small bites at a time. They were aided by confusion and disagreement among the forces they were fighting, but they never permitted themselves to be caught at the far end of a strung-out supply line. In the two decades that followed, the danger of Japanese attack was always present. Moscow did everything possible to create a self-contained Far Eastern army. It was based in Chita and was supplied in major part by food from Mongolia. Industries were built in the east, notably at Komsomolsk-na-Amur, to give the Far Eastern armies a source of ammunition, steel, and heavy metals. New plants were built in the eastern Urals to cut the length of transportation hauls to the Far East. The Trans-Siberian was provided with a network of branch connections and painfully double-tracked.

This paid off when the critical confrontation arose with Japan in 1939, on the eve of World War II. This was only the culmination of a series of battles, skirmishes, and frontier encounters which had been going on for nearly a decade, largely around the perimeter of Mongolia. It had been preceded by a major engagement in the summer of 1938 at Lake Khasan on the Ussuri River line not too distant from the scene of the Soviet-Chinese clashes in the spring of 1969. The Japanese Kwantung army attacked the Russian frontier at Khasan in major strength at the end of June 1938. The Russians were driven back and the Japanese advanced onto Soviet territory. The fighting continued heavily while the Russians mobilized substantial reserves. Finally, in early August 1938, the Russians inflicted a defeat on the Japanese, and both sides returned to their previous positions.

But the following spring the Japanese challenged the Russians much more seriously. The Japanese made a surprise attack May 11, 1939, at Buir-Nur on the eastern frontiers of Mongolia, twelve miles east of the Kalkhin-gol River. The Mongol frontier forces were quickly overrun and the Soviet troops which were rushed to support them were unable to hold the line against the Japanese Sixth Army.

It was apparent that this was not a minor border clash but a full-scale test by the Japanese Kwantung army of the ability of the Russians to defend their Far Eastern lines. (It may have been partly inspired by the support the Russians were then giving the Chinese Nationalists against the Japanese.) The Russians had a considerable force in Mongolia. These troops and Mongol troops under Soviet command were given the job of slowing down the Japanese. Meanwhile, a major Soviet task force was assembled under Georgi K. Zhukov, the future marshal who was to emerge as the leading Soviet commander of World War II. He was then known as a brilliant cavalry and tank officer, deputy commander of the Belorussian military district. In early June he was suddenly summoned to Moscow and on June 2, 1939, ushered into the presence of Klimenti Voroshilov, the Soviet War Commissar. Voroshilov told Zhukov what Zhukov already knew—that the Japanese had suddenly attacked Mongolia in the first days of May. He showed Zhukov a map of the Mongolian frontier and said: "I think this is becoming a serious military adventure. In any case, it is still going on. Can you fly out there immediately and if needed take over command of the troops?"

By the morning of June 5 Zhukov had arrived at Tamsag-Bulak, then as now the military command post for the eastern tip of Mongolia. He quickly learned that the Japanese had attacked in great strength ten to fifteen miles east of the Khalkin-gol near Nomon-khan-Byrd-obo. The Mongol-Soviet forces had fallen back steadily. On May 22 the Japanese renewed the offensive in greater strength.

Zhukov's reaction was characteristic. What he did at the

Khalkin-gol was a dress rehearsal of what he was to do in every great battle he conducted in World War II. First he sacked two or three corps commanders who he believed had not been vigorous enough in opposing the Japanese or as well briefed on the combat situation as needed. Then he gave orders to all forces to hold the line while a powerful strike force was assembled. This was not easy. The Khalkin-gol front was at that time some 400 miles from the nearest railhead. Everything had to be trucked in, and many of the men marched on foot or came by horseback.

Before Zhukov could assemble his strike force he fought a series of sharp air battles in late June, some of the largest air engagements of the time, with upward of 200 or 300 planes engaged. The Japanese lost sixty-four planes between June 22 and 26. The Russian losses were not light, but the Russians established control of the air—an important factor in enabling Zhukov to maintain security in amassing his strike force. He built up his special First Army Group to a strength of thirty-five infantry battalions and twenty cavalry squadrons (as compared with twenty-five infantry battalions and seventeen cavalry squadrons of the Japanese Sixth Army). He had at his disposal nearly 500 tanks, 346 armored cars, and about 500 planes. He had a two-to-one advantage in planes and artillery and a four-to-one edge in armor.

His supply columns brought in 18,000 tons of artillery ammunition, 6,500 tons of air bombs, 15,000 tons of gasoline and oil, 4,000 tons of food products, 7,500 tons of fuel, and 4,000 tons of other heavy freight. He had a fleet of 3,500 trucks and 1,400 tank trucks to supply his forces. It was the largest motor-supply operation the Soviet Army had ever undertaken.

Zhukov enforced rigorous security, a complete ban on radio communications, a ban on movements in forward areas during daylight, a ban on written orders, a ban on officers appearing near front areas with insignia of rank. Officers were not permitted to employ touring cars or jeeps—only trucks, even for reconnaissance.

Tactical surprise was complete. Zhukov's forces jumped off at 5:45 A.M. August 20, 1939, and by August 31 he had driven the Japanese in complete disorder back across the Mongolian frontiers in a classic double envelopment. The Japanese forces had numbered more than 30,000 men, backed by 250 planes, 300 cannon, and 140 tanks. The bulk of the force was wiped out.

Zhukov's operation had been costly but was magnificently successful. The psychological effect on the Japanese was decisive. The Khalkin-gol defeat played a major role in discouraging the Japanese from any military adventures while Russia was so deeply engaged against Hitler in World War II.

The style, tactics and strategy, careful mustering of over-whelmingly decisive forces, extreme secrecy and security, efforts at double envelopment (thirty years after the event Premier Tsedenbal still spoke of the Khalkin-gol battle as "a modern Cannae"), lavish employment of swift-strike forces, heavy concentrations of armor and planes, patient waiting and holding off of enemy attacks until the decisive strength and dispositions had been made—all of these became characteristic of Zhukov's World War II victories in the battles of Moscow, Stalingrad, Kursk-Orel, and Berlin.

They were to provide the model for the next and even more decisive Soviet military campaign in the Far East, the magnificent—but little known in the West—Soviet operation against Japan's Kwantung army at the close of World War II. Stalin had promised Churchill and Roosevelt at Yalta to intervene against Japan within two or three months of the end of the European war. Planning started immediately. The Japanese had about 1.2 million men, 5,000 guns, 1,115 tanks, and 1,200 planes to defend their positions in Manchuria and North China. They were, to be sure, no longer the cream of the Japanese army, but it was no insignificant force. It took the Russians about three months to muster their forces and, in the end, they had to attack before they had completed preparations because the United States had dropped the atom bomb. If Stalin was to get in on the kill of Japan he had little time in which to do it.

Three Soviet fronts were created—the trans-Baikal front and the second and first Far Eastern fronts. The trans-Baikal front comprised four armies, a tank army and a cavalry mechanized group, and the Twelfth Air Army. It was to strike from eastern Mongolia in two columns, one toward the line of the Chinese Eastern Railroad, Tsitsihar, and Harbin, and a second southeast to the South Manchuria Railroad heading for Changchung and Mukden. These forces were commanded by Marshal Rodion Y. Malinovsky. The second Far Eastern front, with three armies and a mechanized corps, was commanded by Army General M. A. Purkayev. It was to strike across the Amur between Blagoveshchensk and Khabarovsk and race the trans-Baikal front for Harbin.

The first Far Eastern front, under Marshal K. A. Meretskov, was to strike west across the Ussuri River from points midway between Khabarovsk and Vladivostok.

In all, the Soviet forces, in general command of Marshal A. M. Vasilevsky, by August 11, 1945, numbered eleven field armies and one tank army—a total of 1,577,725 men, 26,137 guns, 5,556 tanks, and 3,446 planes. The Russians outnumbered the Japanese 1.8 in men, 4.8 in armor, and 1.9 in tanks.

This enormous force required 136,000 railroad cars to move. During June and July 1945 between twenty-two and thirty trains daily were conveying men and munitions east of Lake Baikal.

Half of all the forces were concentrated in the trans-Baikal front, based on Choibalsan in eastern Mongolia with backup bases at Chita and Irkutsk. Headquarters were at Tamsag-Bulak and Matat-Somon in eastern Mongolia.

The plan of campaign called for a series of double envelopments to destroy both the Japanese forces in Manchuria and the

Japanese strategic reserve concentrated in the Peking area in a period of not more than fifteen to twenty days.

The Soviet attack was launched at ten minutes past midnight on August 9 without artillery preparation. On August 14 the Japanese government announced capitulation. The Russians now insist that the Kwantung army would not agree to surrender until August 18–19. The act of surrender was signed at 3:30 P.M., August 19. However, the Russians were not eager to accept an early surrender. They made paratroop drops on Harbin, Mukden, and other Manchurian centers only on August 18. The Soviet troops had advanced up to fifty and more miles a day, often through most difficult mountain and desert terrain, but in spite of their efforts were unable to reach Peking and Port Arthur before the actual Japanese surrender.

The Russian tactics in the Khalkin-gol and August 1945 offensives were basically similar, marked by very rapidly moving armored and mechanized columns, paratroop drops, heavy air support, and, in 1945, extensive use of rocket weapons.

The location of the chief army groups, the direction of their strikes, and the weight of concentration in eastern Mongolia and on the Amur and Ussuri all match the pattern of Soviet military needs for a strike against the Chinese. The Chinese defense forces are concentrated in precisely those areas where the Japanese Kwantung army was located. The Russian build-ups have gone forward in precisely those regions which marked the 1939 and 1945 build-ups.

The only new feature of the Soviet plans relates to new weaponry, new long-range missiles, and nuclear arms. The range of the installations in Mongolia is great enough to cover all the targets in Inner Mongolia, the provinces to the west, and the Peking region, if not farther.

The only apparent new factor in Soviet dispositions is the concentration in southern Mongolia on the edge of the Gobi.

If Soviet war plans for China follow the patterns of those

against the Japanese on the same terrain (and there is no reason for any essential difference), they call for a quick strike at the key industrial and port areas of Manchuria, the Peking region, the principal centers of Inner Mongolia, and North China. The Soviet timetable, unless it markedly diverges from those of past operations, calls for a blitz attack timed to require not more than a fortnight and quite possibly as little as ten days. Its aim is the paralyzing of the main centers of Chinese resistance and control preceded by a neutralizing strike to immobilize and destroy the Chinese nuclear capability. With the advance in military technology in the twenty-five years since Russia fought Japan, it would be expected that the primitive air drops which marked the end of the Soviet attack on the Kwantung army would be replaced by quick airlifts and drops to the major Chinese centers as soon as the Chinese nuclear potential had been destroyed.

There is no indication in the general philosophy of Soviet military doctrine of plans for a large-scale general land war in which Soviet forces would fight mass battles with the Chinese. The emphasis, as in the doctrine which has marked Soviet military thinking since before World War II, is on a swift overwhelming strike which paralyzes the enemy and reduces him to the state of surrender within days. The 1945 attack on the Kwantung army with its ten-day capitulation provides a classic of contemporary Soviet military thinking.

Given the state of Soviet military technology, the Soviet general staff should be prepared to guarantee the Kremlin that a knockout of China could be achieved by means of a surprise lightning blow, using nuclear weapons, within a matter of days.

To most Americans the actual use of nuclear weapons in war has become almost unthinkable. It has become unthinkable to most Russians—as far as the United States is concerned. But not with China. One of the most respected of Soviet scientists told his American colleagues in the spring of 1969 that Russians were fed up with China and that war was not unlikely.

"When we go to war we will not fight with our little fingers like you Americans," he said. "We will be fighting to the death."

He left no doubt that he meant nuclear arms would be used against China.

It seems beyond question that the war the Russians plan against China is such a war as the world has never before seen, employing hydrogen as well as atom bombs—not as the United States did in World War II in isolated "demonstrations," but as calculated weapons of utter destruction, designed to reduce China in the quickest possible time to complete surrender. The theory that the Russian Far Eastern strategy is basically missile-nuclear received substantial support in August 1969 when Colonel-General Vladimir F. Tolubko, first Deputy Commander of Soviet Strategic Rocket Forces, was named commander in chief of Soviet Far Eastern forces.

The Sino-Soviet war, if it comes, promises to be the world's first nuclear war.

CHAPTER XI

Long Live the Victory of the People's War

The ninth Congress of the Chinese Communist Party ended April 24, 1969, in Peking after more than three weeks of speeches, debate, and decisions, among them the approval of the nomination of Lin Piao, Minister of Defense, as heir apparent to Mao Tse-tung. The action made formal what many had been aware of from the moment Lin Piao took over command of China's armed forces in 1959—that he was, in effect, Mao's alter ego.

Three days later Peking made public a 24,000-word thesis by Lin Piao, setting forth China's position on the major issues of the day and, specifically, on the question of war with the Soviet Union.

Said Lin Piao:

We must on no account relax our revolutionary vigilance because of victory and on no account ignore the danger of U.S. imperialism and Soviet revisionism launching a large-scale war of aggression.

We must make full preparations, preparations against their launching a big war and against their launching a war at an early date, preparations against their launching a conventional war and against their launching a large-scale nuclear war.

In short we must be prepared. . . .

If they insist on fighting, we will keep them company and fight to the finish. The Chinese Revolution won out on the battlefield.

Armed with Mao Tse-tung's thought, tempered in the Great Proletarian Cultural Revolution, and with full confidence in victory, the Chinese people, in their hundreds of millions, and the Chinese People's Liberation Army are determined to liberate their sacred territory Taiwan and resolutely, thoroughly, wholly and completely wipe out all aggressors who dare to come.

Lin Piao supported his view with a new quotation from Chairman Mao, apparently part of a speech delivered at the Congress, although no text had been issued:

Working hand in glove, Soviet revisionism and U.S. imperialism have done so many foul and evil things that the revolutionary people the world over will not let them go unpunished. The people of all countries are rising. A new historical period of opposing U.S. imperialism and Soviet revisionism has begun.

With regard to the question of world war, there are but two possibilities: One is that the war will give rise to revolution and the other is that revolution will prevent the war.

The remarks of Lin Piao and Mao Tse-tung made plain that the ninth Party Congress had squarely faced the question of war with the Soviet Union and the probability that this would, in fact, be a nuclear war.

Peking commentaries since the ninth Party Congress are based on the assumption, as the *Peking Review* put it, that the

Soviet Union is actively preparing for war, constructing air force and guided-missile bases along both the Sino-Soviet and Sino-Mongolian borders. The Russians themselves, the Chinese commentaries note, insist that their main weapons are "missiles with nuclear warheads of unlimited destructive power." Soviet guided-missile units stand in battle array in trans-Baikalian Siberia and Mongolia, ready to attack China at any moment.

How China proposes to respond to the Russians and specifically to a Soviet nuclear blitz is no secret. The outline of Chinese defense plans was placed on record by Lin Piao on September 2, 1965, in a speech commemorating the twentieth anniversary of China's victory over Japan. While the main thrust of Lin Piao's remarks, as might be expected at that time, was addressed to the United States, every word he spoke about a U.S. attack applies with equal force to the Soviet Union and to the present nuclear threat.

Lin Piao's remarks were made shortly before China herself acquired nuclear capability, but this fact merely adds weight to his description of China's tactics. The answer to nuclear threat, said Lin Piao, is the "people's war":

> A people's war inevitably meets with many difficulties, with ups and downs and setbacks in the course of its development, but no force can alter its general trend toward inevitable triumph. . . .
> The poorly armed have defeated the better armed. People's armed forces, beginning with only primitive swords, spears, rifles, hand grenades, have in the end defeated the imperialist forces armed with modern airplanes, tanks, heavy artillery, and atom bombs. Guerrilla forces have ultimately defeated regular armies. "Amateurs" who were never trained in any military schools have eventually defeated "professionals" graduated from military academies. And so on and so forth. Things stubbornly develop in a way that runs counter to the assertions of the revisionists [Lin Piao's word for Moscow] and facts are slapping them in the face.

Lin Piao contended that Moscow believed that a nation without nuclear arms (as China then was) was incapable of defeating an enemy with nuclear weapons, no matter what methods it adopted. "Their line in army building," he observed, "is the bourgeois line which ignores the human factor and sees only the material factor and which regards technique as everything and politics as nothing."

In contrast, the Chinese "never take a gloomy view of war."

Peking's attitude has always been clear on wars of aggression:

> First, we are against them, and secondly, we are not afraid of them. We will destroy whoever attacks us.
>
> The revolutionary people of the world will sweep away everything that stands in the way of their advance. Khrushchev is finished. And the successors to Khrushchev's revisionism [the present Kosygin-Brezhnev regime] will fare no better than the imperialists, the reactionaries, and the Khrushchev revisionists who have all set themselves against the people's war, will be swept like dust from the stage of history by the mighty broom of the revolutionary people.

Speaking to the United States in words equally applicable to Russia, Lin Piao said:

> The vast ocean of several hundred million Chinese people in arms will be more than enough to submerge your few million aggressor troops. If you dare to impose war on us we shall gain freedom of action. It will then not be up to you to decide how the war will be fought. We shall fight in the ways most advantageous to us to destroy the enemy and wherever the enemy can be most easily destroyed.
>
> Since the Chinese people were able to destroy the Japanese aggressors twenty years ago they are certainly still capable of finishing off the U.S. [read: Russian] aggressors today. The naval and air superiority you boast about cannot intimidate the Chinese people and neither can the atom bomb you brandish at us. If you want to send troops go ahead, the more the better.

We will annhilate as many as you can send and can even give you receipts.

This may seem like mere rhetoric, but Lin Piao was actually setting the philosophical framework within which to fit Chinese strategy and tactics when confronted with nuclear war and a technologically superior opponent. His theories are, of course, based on the strategy and tactics which Mao Tse-tung originated in the course of the long struggle against the Japanese during the 1930's and 1940's. At that time the Chinese Communists were far weaker, comparatively speaking, relative to the Japanese than they now are relative to either the United States or Russia.

Mao's strategic rule for his Eighth Route and New Fourth armies was: "Guerrilla warfare is basic but lose no chance for mobile warfare under favorable conditions."

"Guerrilla warfare," Lin Piao contended, "is the only way to mobilize and apply the whole strength of the people against the enemy, the only way to expand our forces in the course of the war, to deplete and weaken the enemy, gradually change the balance of forces between the enemy and ourselves, switch from guerrilla to mobile warfare, and finally defeat the enemy."

He cited Mao's famous dictum: "The enemy advances, we retreat; the enemy camps, we harass; the enemy tires, we attack; the enemy retreats, we pursue."

Everyone joined in the war against Japan—troops, civilian men and women, old and young, every single village. Ingenious methods were devised—sparrow warfare (hit-and-run tactics by groups of two or three guerrillas), landmines, tunnel warfare, sabotage, and guerrilla operations on lakes and rivers.

The aim, said Lin Piao, must always be to entice or entrap the enemy into a battle of annhilation, always seeking to concentrate an absolutely superior force (two, three, four, and even five or six times as strong as the enemy). He quoted Mao once more:

We should first attack dispersed or isolated enemy forces and only attack concentrated and strong enemy forces later; we should strive to wipe out the enemy through mobile warfare; we should fight no battle unprepared and fight no battle we are not sure of winning; in any battle we fight we should develop our army's strong points and its excellent style of fighting.

To annihilate the enemy we must adopt the policy of luring him in deep and abandon some cities and districts of our own accord in a planned way to let him in. It is only after letting the enemy in that people can take part in the war in various ways. We must let the enemy become elated, stretch out all his ten fingers, and become hopelessly bogged down. Thus, we can concentrate superior forces to destroy the enemy forces one by one, to eat them out mouthful by mouthful. Only by wiping out the enemy's effective strength can cities and localities be finally held or seized.

Lin Piao noted that in eight years of fighting against the Japanese the Communist forces fought more than 125,000 engagements and put more than 1.7 million Japanese and puppet troops out of action. In fighting the Nationalists, the Communists destroyed more than 8 million Kuomintang troops.

The key to Lin Piao's formula was contained in a single paragraph:

"However highly developed modern weapons and technical equipment may be and however complicated the methods of modern warfare in the final analysis, the outcome of a war will be decided by the sustained fighting of the ground forces, by the fighting at close quarters on battlefields, by the political consciousness of the men, by their courage and spirit of sacrifice."

In other words, hand-to-hand combat.

Lin Piao's words are backed up by Chinese Red Army manuals and the manuals employed in training civil-defense forces (the whole Chinese public) stressing close combat—the bayonet, the knife, the hand grenade, the ax, the pick. By learning to fight hand to hand, by learning to hold fire until the enemy actually appeared before you, the manuals stressed, the enemy's advantage in technology was nullified. In the end, whatever he did, the enemy must come in and seize the ground. The Chinese people were trained to hold the ground as did the men at the Battle of Lexington—not to fire until they could see the whites of the enemy's eyes. No easy task. One requiring courage and confidence. The People's Liberation Army was (and is) trained constantly in night fighting, in guerrilla tactics, in mountain, jungle, and forest combat. It is accustomed to walking to the battle site and living off the countryside.

Lin Piao said with pride that the Chinese armed forces were the equal of any in the world—up to the distance of 200 meters. What he meant was that whenever the Chinese could entice the enemy to fight hand to hand the Chinese would win.

These were the tactics which wore down the Japanese year after year. This, the Chinese insisted, was what won. They would have none of the Americans' argument that U.S. power turned the balance against Japan or the Russians' that it was their army which defeated Japan on the mainland. The Chinese were confident that their tactics had wrecked the Japanese. This was what would wreck anyone who tried to seize the mainland again.

What would happen when and if Russia attacked? The first act, clearly, would be nuclear. As far as unclassified Western intelligence is concerned, China has two principal sources of nuclear weapons—the Lanchow reactor, a gaseous diffusion plant estimated to produce enough fissionable material to make about fifty bombs a year, and Paotow, with two small reactors possibly capable of turning out materials for a dozen bombs a year. Assuming that Chinese production has been constant and increasing since early 1900, they might by 1970 have a stock of 200 nuclear weapons or a few more—basically atomic bombs, but they have been making hydrogen weapons for at least three years.

As for delivery capability, the Chinese produced their first missiles of 450- to 650-mile range as early as 1963. By 1966 they were up to 1,200 miles, and in 1969 they were on the verge of intercontinental capability. This does not mean they have a large store of these weapons, but enough missiles to mount a nuclear threat against Russian Far Eastern centers, Vladivostok, Nakhodka, Blagoveshchensk, Komsomolsk-na-Amur, Chita, Irkutsk, and the Bratsk power complex. They have the capability of wiping out or badly damaging Soviet concentrations in eastern Mongolia based in Choibalsan, the southern Gobi, and Ulan Bator.

Whether the Chinese have installed missiles directed against all these targets has not been confirmed by any overt intelligence, but the presumption on which Soviet plans are being made is that China has done just that. In view of China's certainty that Russia would use the bomb in case of war the presumption seems sensible.

Thus it is an intelligent guess that nuclear missiles are in place on the Chinese as well as the Russian side. The first act in the war would be an effort to cripple each other's nuclear capability. If the Russian first strike was successful the highly mobile Soviet panzers would snake across the frontier, striking for the key North China and Manchurian centers.

The Soviet military is operating on the presumption that a paralyzing nuclear blow and a quick armored blitz would knock China out of the war in a matter of days. But Lin Piao's answer is that this would only be the opening phase of a people's war such as was mounted against Japan, the first days of what might well become a hundred-year war, a war in which the Chinese would remorselessly and endlessly grind down, exhaust, and annihilate wave after wave of Russians sent in to try to hold the ground "at a distance of 200 meters."

Nor is Lin Piao's tactic a new one, despite his crediting of the military doctrine to Mao Tse-tung. It is, in fact, the traditional Chinese tactic when confronted by an enemy more scientifically, industrially, or technologically advanced than herself. She has for thousands of years permitted the enemy to advance into the country if she could not halt him, and then, by all the means of superior Chinese culture, civilization, and manpower, suffocated and drowned him.

Long before World War II and Japan's fateful adventures in the Pacific, her best and most acute military leaders had come to fear that the task of occupying and subduing the vast human mass of China was so gigantic that it was beyond the limited human and material resources of Japan.

Precisely such a prospect faced the Russians in the phase of the war which would follow the initial nuclear strike. The People's Liberation Army today numbers 3 million men, more or less, plus a militia force of 7 to 12 million and possibly fifteen divisions of special border troops. This is substantially larger than the force available to the Russians in the Far East and Mongolia. The Soviet force east of the Urals is estimated at above a million, of whom 100,000 to 200,000 are in Mongolia. The actual Mongol army probably numbers another 100,000. The Chinese forces available in the Inner Mongolia-Manchuria-North China triangle hold a 1.5 to 1.8 ratio of superiority over the Russians in manpower.

The Chinese have been trained in survival against nuclear attack, but whether the Chinese measures will, in fact, prove effective no one can be certain until the test comes. An elaborate honeycomb system under which each small region of the country is to be self-sufficient in supply and defense has been in existence for several years. In theory, even if all communications between cells or with the center have been wiped out survival will be possible. The cells have been trained to seek shelter in hills, caves, and dugouts until the enemy actually appears "within a distance of 200 meters." Then they will give combat at a range at which neither nuclear weapons, supersonic aircraft, nor high-speed armored vehicles are of value.

Mao is quoted by the Russians as saying that 300 million Chinese might be killed in a nuclear war, but China would not be wiped out. Based on present population estimates, if the Russians should conceivably kill 300 million Chinese—which would mean an all-out attack on the principal Chinese population centers—there would still, incredibly, be 500 million or perhaps 600 million Chinese alive and prepared to carry on the battle, according to Mao's plans.

Thus, even after killing more human beings that ever have been slaughtered in human combat in history, the Russians would still confront a numerical inferiority ratio of possibly three to one; they would still be confronted with a task greater than their manpower or economy could endure, the task of attempting to occupy all of China, fighting, over and over again, against the cell-like defense units, carrying on combat at "200 meters."

No Russian government could face such a possibility; the prospect would bring the Soviet people up in arms against Moscow. Not even their chauvinism against the Chinese would swing them to support the prospect of the world's greatest nuclear war followed by a hundred years of attempting to subdue a population of 500 or 600 million in endless combat.

No such war plan, it is certain, has been drafted by the Soviet high command or is contemplated by the Kremlin. All the Soviet military projections are based on an entirely different calculation: the conviction that if the Chinese nuclear retaliatory capability is taken out and her principal North China, Manchurian, and Inner Mongolian cities are seized the "usurper" government of the "renegade adventurist"—Mao—will fall and his place will be taken by genuine Communists friendly to Moscow, loyal to the principles of Marxism-Leninism as preached and practiced by the Soviet Union, true Communist elements from whom Mao seized power and who wait in the wings for an opportunity to respond to the national call of China and take the helm.

The Russian calculation almost certainly is based on the same gross misjudgment of popular and national political currents which has characterized Soviet thinking, almost consistently, since the earliest days of the Bolshevik uprising—the inability to assess, weigh, and interpret nationalist feelings and the strength of nationalism as a political force in other countries.

Just as the Kremlin was unable to assess accurately the relative political forces in Czechoslovakia, so they are unable to assess the politics of China and to postulate what would happen in event of an attack on China. They rely on chauvinism in their own country as a factor in uniting Russia against China; they do not understand that nationalism and chauvinism are infinitely more powerful in China and have been stimulated to fever pitch by the Communist revolution and its successes (as seen by the Chinese) in Korea, in India, and in opposing the United States and Russia.

Moscow is unable to understand that their plans for war against China differs little in concept (only in the new technology) from those of the Japanese. Moscow is certain, therefore, to evoke the same kind of popular response in China, a rallying of national consciousness and a unifying of the popular will—the arousing, as Lin Piao puts it, of those forces which give birth to the people's war.

China does not have the modern arms of Russia. Her nuclear arsenal is limited. Her missiles have less range than the Soviet. She does not possess the supersonic Soviet aircraft, the array of rocket weapons, the armor, the electronic gear, the guidance systems, the communications network.

But she has manpower. She has a morale factor which runs much higher than the Russian. The Russians do not want to fight a war—not the ordinary Russians. They may hate the Chinese and fear them, but they fear war more. Not so the Chinese. Unlike the Russian he has little to lose materially by war. He is nearer to revolution and revolutionary sacrifice. The younger generation, just emerging from the Cultural Revolution, has been trained in battle, hardship, sacrifice. That, many Chinese feel, was the real meaning of the Cultural Revolution—the blooding of the young, the revival in them of the spirit of hard combat, war, readiness to fight against any odds, be it Russia or the United States, be it tanks or nuclear bombs.

In the Chinese propaganda film *The Anti-Chinese Crimes of the New Czars*, ordinary fishermen are shown in cockleshell boats armed only with poles, standing firm against the sleek armored gunboats and heavy cannon of the Russians. The Chinese are fearless and unshaken no matter how heavy the odds. Simple Chinese peasants stand up in winter against the most modern Soviet tanks. Armed only with sticks, they beat at the steel vehicles and do not give their ground, even when the heavy vehicles turn and grind them under their steel treads. The film glorifies the simple man armed with the simplest of weapons doing battle with courage and boldness against the most powerful of Russian arms. In the end victory goes to the Chinese.

No one, in advance, can accurately estimate the unestimable —the factor of human spirit, of morale, of vitality, of willingness to battle, to sacrifice, to die. No one can calculate the weight of this factor multiplied 600 million times or 900 million times.

But no one facing that calculation could feel great confidence in the assurances of the Soviet generals that a ten-day nuclear blitz will give the Kremlin full victory and success in China. The fact may be that the ten-day nuclear blitz will prove to be only the opening stage of a century of war. In the dark days of the war against Japan the Chinese used to console themselves with a grim joke.

One Chinese asks the other about the results of the last battle against the Japanese.

"We lost 10,000 men," says the Chinese.

"How many did the Japanese lose?"

"One hundred."

"Marvelous," says the Chinese. "We'll soon have them on the run."

CHAPTER XII

Hitler

versus Hitler

Americans still ask the question: How can Communists fight Communists? How can Moscow fight Peking? They forget or never have learned that Communists historically have always fought each other—frequently they have devoted themselves so completely to fighting each other they have had no time to fight anyone else.

Karl Marx broke with every other leader of socialist thought. He preferred to stand alone without supporters rather than yield on any point of what he called principle. Only Engels stood with Marx throughout his active career and there were times when even Marx and Engels disagreed.

Lenin followed in Marx's mode. He broke with Plekhanov, the founder of the Marxist party in Russia, and with almost every other Marxist. He fought his Communist enemies far more savagely than the Russian Czar. The Second International fought the First International, and the Third International (founded by

Lenin) fought everyone. Stalin fought all Communists of any standing in Russia and killed as many as he could. It was war to the death against the Trotskyite Communists, the Right Opposition Communists, the Left Opposition Communists. And, of course, Lenin had stamped out every Marxist party in Russia but his own.

The idea that there is something odd, unusual, unreal about combat between Communists is too naïve for belief. Stalin killed far more Communists than non-Communists. He fought Tito in Yugoslavia, who fought back, successfully. Then, fearing more Titos, Stalin had most of the remaining Communist chiefs of state shot and replaced by police dummies.

The battles of the Communists are more savage than any other battles. Stalin was able to make a pact with Hitler and did all he could to keep it. But he devoted a lifetime to plotting and opposing other Communists—Trotsky until Trotsky was murdered and Mao after Mao came to power.

What lends special ferocity to the battle of Communist against Communist is the quasireligious quality of doctrine and belief. The Communists, particularly those of Russia and China, are trained to believe that the doctrine as espoused, say, by Stalin is the true word and that anyone who challenges this true word is an unbeliever or, worse, an apostate. In China the religious quality goes even further, as anyone who has seen the phenomenon of Chairman Mao's little red book is aware. Fishermen, before getting into their boats, read the little red book. Soldiers going into battle hold the little red book high above their heads like a holy relic. Doctors about to perform an operation study the little red book while giving anesthesia. When the battle is won, the catch is seined, the operation is completed, the Chinese, little red book in hand, sing "The East Is Red" like a religious hymn.

Once conflict and controversy begin between Communists there is little that can be done toward compromise, for how can a true believer break bread with the infidel? It is this quality of the medieval religious war which gives to the Sino-Soviet quarrel its schismatic, syndical, Talmudic quality, its atmosphere of argument over the number of angels who can dance on the head of a pin. Each side brings this element to the conflict—Mao, the image of the father, of the sun, of the celestial kingdom, the being higher than human whose simple word can inspire the common man to move mountains or exceed his quota for catching fish. In the propaganda films Mao's image is flashed on the screen again and again, constantly infusing strength and belief in the masses. Mao has his holy princes like Lin Piao to spread the word and wield the sword of doctrine, swift and flashing, and his ordinary worshipers, the little people who repeat the Name many times in the course of the day, drawing strength and comfort from it.

On the Russian side the purity of doctrine is badly impaired by the half century since its inspirer, Lenin, walked the earth, and by the semirepudiation of his first disciple, Stalin. The interim has been filled with less than perfect ministers and the flock has badly fallen from grace. But high priests like ideologue Mikhail Suslov and his acolytes still search the ancient texts and extract appropriate citations to bring down anathema upon the heathen apostates of the East. No missionary carrying a vision of the Western deity to the non-Christians of Asia bristles more with the might of doctrine than the scholars of the Institute of Marxism-Leninism in Moscow as they brandish the holy texts over the infidel.

The real question is not why the Communists fight but by what means are they now fighting and what stage has the battle reached?

Long since each side has begun to see the other as a kind of reincarnation of Hitler—the modern devil. Thus Lin Piao calls the "Soviet revisionist renegade clique" not only "the new czars" but "social imperialists" striving to simulate the "new order" of Europe of Hitler, the "greater east co-prosperity sphere" of Japa-

nese militarism and the "free-world community" of the United
States.

Russia has been transformed, in Lin Piao's words, from "the
world's first state of the dictatorship of the proletariat into a dark,
fascist state of the dictatorship of the bourgeoisie."

The Russian fascists, Lin Piao declares, have evoked a philosophy to serve their purposes. Thus they are trying to convert
the whole of the Communist world into a "socialist community"
which, in fact, would be a Russian colonial domain. To mask this
purpose they have invented a theory of "limited sovereignty"
which gives them the asserted right to intervene in any country
as they please.

"What does all this stuff mean?" Lin Piao demands. "It
means that your sovereignty is 'limited' while his is unlimited.
You won't obey him? He will exercise 'international dictatorship'
over you, dictatorship over the peoples of other countries in order
to form the 'socialist community' ruled by the new czars."

When Russian Communists talk of "fraternal parties" they
actually, in Lin Piao's view, "regard themselves as the 'Patriarchi-
cal Party' and as the new Czar, who is free to invade and occupy
the territory of other countries."

The Chinese do not limit themselves to opposing the Russians ideologically; they advance themselves as the supporters of
the national Czech cause. Although China actually is violently
opposed to the philosophy of the Czech liberals, she supports
Czecholosovakia against Russia. The Chinese support all countries which they believe the Russians are attempting to subvert
and oppress. They offer support to the Mongols against the Russians (and against the Mongol government). They support
Communist parties and fractions of parties anywhere in the world
that oppose the Russians.

Most significantly, they support "the proletariat and the
laboring people of the Soviet Union in their just struggle to overthrow the Soviet revisionist renegade clique" and they support

the peoples of other countries—not merely Czechoslovakia—in "their just struggle against Soviet revisionist social-imperialism."

In other words, China has raised the flag of revolution in Russia itself and gives the struggle against the Russians and their influence in any country, socialist or otherwise, and in any form the same order of priority as the struggle of backward and colonial peoples against so-called American imperialism.

As far as the Soviet Union is concerned, the Chinese have raised again the famous slogan of Lenin and his Bolsheviks that "Russia is a prisonhouse of peoples."

They have taken up the banner of support for all of the hundred minority nationalities in the Soviet Union, which, they assert, are being "ruthlessly oppressed and exploited."

"Their national languages are subjected to all sort of discrimination, their national culture is being suppressed unscrupulously, and their national history is arbitrarily adulterated and distorted. They are crudely deprived of the minimum rights of national autonomy," the Chinese contend. The Russians have uprooted many national minorities from their traditional lands and are suppressing opposition with troops, police, and secret agents, creating "an atmosphere of white terror."

The minority struggles in Russia, the Chinese contend, gave rise to rebellions in 1962 in the Ukraine, Uzbekistan, and southern Siberia which were quelled by armed force and in which many were shot and killed. New uprisings occurred in the Ukraine in 1963 and in Azerbaijan in 1965. A major outbreak arose in Chimkent, southern Kazakhstan, in 1967 in which several dozen demonstrators were killed.

Unrest in the Ukraine in 1967 produced a wave of arrests in Kiev and Odessa, and in 1968 there were "large-scale revolutionary mass movements" in Kazakhstan, Taishet, and Tulun which were "barbarously suppressed" by Soviet troops.

The Chinese have made a special point of support for the Tartar minority in Russia which traditionally has been subjected to very rigorous repression, having been uprooted en masse from the Crimea at the end of World War II for alleged pro-German tendencies and shipped to Central Asia and Siberia. The fight of the Crimean Tartars for basic civil rights and redress of their wrongs has attracted the support of many vigorous Soviet liberals, including General Grigorenko, who in the spring of 1969 was arrested in Tashkent while attempting to aid the Tartar movement.

The Chinese have protested the treatment of the Tartars, widely publicizing the efforts of the "Soviet revisionist new czars" to quell Tartar uprisings with police, security brigades, and fire units. Peking contends that Tartar delegates who went to Moscow to protest conditions were beaten at the entrance to the Communist Party Central Committee building in Staryaya Ploshad and arrested before they were able to deliver their complaints. The Tartars, of course, are the remnants of the Mongols.

The Chinese have manifested sympathy for nationalist movements in the Baltic states, although they are aware that most of these people have right-wing, non-Communist leanings.

The Chinese do not limit themselves to expressions of interest and sympathy. They take the line that the "suppressed nations in the Soviet Union" have a "glorious revolutionary tradition" and they support the struggle of the nationalities to overthrow the Moscow regime. Peking has expressed confidence that the nationalities will succeed in this task and win emancipation from "the new czars."

While it was the savage outbreak on the Ussuri River on March 2, 1969, which focused new attention on the critical tensions between the Russians and the Chinese, this was, in fact, merely a sharper and more bloody incident in a stream of border incidents—4,189 by Chinese count between October 15, 1964, and March 16, 1969, and perhaps 1,500 between 1960 and 1964.

Each side blames the other for the Ussuri fighting, but the evidence of China's propaganda films indicates that the Chinese have tended to be very provocative in border clashes with self-disciplined, well-trained Soviet border forces. The first two Ussuri battles of March 2 and March 4 were victories for the Chinese. Several score Russian border guards were killed. The March 15 clash was a Soviet reprisal and warning. The Russians moved up heavy missile units and launched a sharp but brief barrage deep into Chinese territory, inflicting several hundred casualties. The warning was explicit: more border skirmishes will bring more heavy bombardments. The fighting died down along the Ussuri, only to flare up in other areas.

What lay behind the Ussuri fighting? Was it a deliberate effort by the Chinese to create an incident and raise international tension on the even of the ninth Party Congress in Peking? Not likely. The conduct of the Chinese in their border altercations with the Russians reveals their state of high emotional passion. It is a simple step from violent argument to an exchange of blows to an exchange of shots.

This view is flatly rejected by the Russians.

Konstantin Simonov, the famous war correspondent who was sent to the Ussuri, which he had known during the fighting with Japan in 1938 and 1939, reached a conclusion shared by most of his countrymen:

> Everything began with a murder.
> Far be it for me to think that those two or three hundred Chinese soldiers who lay in ambush that first March night on Damansky island or those twenty or thirty Chinese soldiers who came out onto the ice that morning became murderers of their own free will.
> In such cases, no killing is done without orders from above. I am perfectly sure that the order to kill was not given by the commander of the Chinese frontier post, nor by the commander of their frontier service, nor even by the commander of their military area.
> I am perfectly sure that the order to kill was handed down from above, from the highest authority of all. . . .

What is to be done not with them but with those who gave that first order before the start of the Damansky events? What measure of evil should be used to assess their actions, both those already committed and those which they are, perhaps, planning for the future?

This view is shared by Premier Tsedenbal of Mongolia: the order to fire was given by Mao; no one below that rank would have taken the responsibility.

The view of Simonov and Tsedenbal is common within the highest circles of the Soviet government. There is no doubt in those quarters that Mao ordered the shooting, deliberately causing an attack that took the lives of Soviet soldiers.

Why is Mao taking this course? Because, once again to quote Mr. Tsedenbal, Mao has approved "arrangements aimed at preparing war against the Soviet Union and other socialist countries." Mao has attacked Russia because it serves his overall policy and prepares his people for the war which, on a limited basis, has already begun.

So far as Mongolia is concerned, Premier Tsedenbal is convinced that Mao long ago opened his attack upon that country and its regime, seeking deliberately to sow discord, overturn the government, and place his own agents in charge. Along the Mongol frontiers incident has followed incident, incitement has followed incitement.

The Chinese people have been infused with the idea of the inevitability of war with Russia, Tsedenbal feels, and the Chinese are employing every possible method to sow discord in Russia and among Russian friends and allies.

To Tsedenbal the Mao policy toward Mongolia is simply an extension of old Chinese Nationalist policy—that is, an effort to resume Chinese control over the country.

Premier Tsedenbal declared: "Speaking of the expansionist policy of Peking, we do not have in mind an imaginary threat now and then arising in the imaginations of individuals as a result of an erroneous evaluation of activities or allegorical reaction to questions concerning sovereignty and independence. We are speaking of a really existent threat coming from the ruling Chinese circles which is aimed primarily against countries neighboring China."

A similar view is taken of China by Soviet Premier Brezhnev, who characterizes Mao Tse-tung's policy as calling "not for a struggle against war, but on the contrary, for war itself which it regards as a positive historical phenomenon."

The objective of China's war policy is the Soviet Union, Brezhnev contends, quoting the Chinese press as appealing to the people to "prepare to wage both a conventional and a large-scale nuclear war against Soviet revisionism."

He told the assembly of Communist parties in Moscow in June 1969:

> The idea of China's Messianic role is being instilled in Chinese workers and peasants. Mass indoctrination in the spirit of chauvinism and vicious anti-Sovietism is under way. Children are being taught geography from textbooks and maps that assign the land of other countries to the Chinese State. "Go hungry and prepare for war"—this is the guideline the Chinese people are being given now.
>
> In so doing no doubt is left as to just what kind of war is meant.
>
> In the light of all this the policy of militarization of China takes on special meaning. We cannot help but compare the feverish military preparations with the fanning of chauvinistic sentiments hostile to the socialist countries, and the overall approach of China's leaders to the problems of war and peace in the present epoch.

The Chinese, in Brezhnev's view, not only are openly preparing their people to wage nuclear and conventional war against Russia, but they are seeking to undermine Soviet influence in every part of the world; setting up "subversive" and schismatic groups in "almost thirty countries," presumably including the

Soviet Union; attempting to split or take over peace groups, youth movements, scientific, and trade-union groups long controlled by the Soviet Union; seeking to intimidate and blackmail Soviet allies.

All this and constant border provocations—130 in the last six months along the Amur and the Ussuri, according to Party leader Aleksei Shtykov of Khabarovsk.

This led Soviet Foreign Minister Andrei Gromyko to observe: "Even our most rabid enemies have never used such unworthy methods and on such a scale as the Chinese leaders are now doing in order to discredit the activities of the Soviet Union and other countries in the socialist community and their peaceable foreign policy."

Despite massive evidence of preparations for war, some diplomats who are thoroughly familiar with Soviet policy challenge the conclusion that Russia will, in fact, wage war on her erstwhile Communist ally. They take the view that the Kremlin would be fearful of political repercussions inside the Soviet Union and that even if the Soviet military recommended preventive war the Politburo would not risk such a dangerous policy. The military, they note, traditionally has been the servants of the executors, not the initiator of Soviet policy. Communism is said to have a long and active tradition against "Bonapartism."

The political facts of contemporary Soviet life, however, contrast deeply with this traditionalist view. The leadership of Brezhnev and Kosygin has consistently displayed weakness in grappling with domestic problems. It confronts mounting internal tensions—a declining economy, a stagnant agriculture, inability to produce sufficient consumer goods to meet demands, a constantly exacerbating struggle with intellectuals and liberals demanding greater freedoms—and has shown no ability to cope with these problems. Its only popular policies are chauvinistic—the general (as distinguished from the intellectual) Russian response to the military action in Czechoslovakia was positive.

Chauvinism toward China evokes enthusiasm across the board—from peasants to cultured scientists, from inmates of concentration camps to disaffected poets.

Thus the incentive to pursue a belligerent policy toward China for purely domestic political reasons is strong, not weak. Some shrewd observers within Russia have been comparing the present Soviet leadership to that of Nicholas II at the time of the Russo-Japanese war: the Soviet leaders welcome a foreign diversion in hope that it will unify the country behind them on a patriotic basis.

As for military influence, there have been increasing signs that traditional barriers against "Bonapartism" have been coming down. The political leadership allied itself with Marshal Zhukov and the army to bring down Lavrenti P. Beria and the secret-police apparatus in 1953. Nikita Khrushchev allied himself with Marshal Zhukov in 1957 to defeat his associates who wanted to oust him from the Politburo. Brezhnev, Kosygin & Co. had the support of the armed forces in disposing of Khrushchev. The military influence in the Czech crisis in 1968 was obvious—it was the generals who insisted that the tanks go in. The military influence in relations with China is equally apparent.

Most of the so-called arguments against "Bonapartism" are specious. The Communist regime since its establishment by Lenin has placed the highest value upon the military and military accomplishments. The Party leadership has prided itself on military discipline, tactics, and strategy. The tradition of both the Soviet and Chinese parties is one of military action. Neither side has ever been hesitant to use weapons. Mao's doctrine that "all power flows from the barrel of the gun" finds no contrary arguments on the Soviet side of the frontier.

Any thought that the military does not weigh more and more heavily in the Soviet inner circle is quickly dispelled by a few weeks' reading of *Pravda* and *Izvestia*. No one is so honored, no one receives so much attention, no one is so respected as the military. When the great conclaves meet in Red Square or in the Kremlin Palace of Soviets, military leaders share at least half the prominent places. The generals and marshals have their own limousines, their own closed stores, their own private-estate communities. They have their own rules of propriety. No colonel is permitted to appear in public carrying a package. And every Russian knows that the only place in a queue for a colonel or a general (or a colonel or a general's wife) is at the head of the line. No general officer is permitted to sit in the balcony of a theater, only in the boxes or stalls.

The idea that there might be a "civilian" party within the government which would argue against a military solution in the Far East is simply not in accord with Soviet reality.

The Soviet Union has not limited itself to military preparations to meet the Chinese threat or to efforts to line up support within the Communist world. It has been active diplomatically in three general areas: Central and Eastern Europe, in an effort to secure the European flank in event of war in the Far East; the United States, in an effort to secure American neutrality or support in event of war with China; and in Asia, in an effort to win influence and establish a new general-security system directed against China.

Russia's diplomatic offensive in Asia has been underway for nearly fifteen years. India was the main target at first and remains the most important objective. Indonesia once ranked number two, but with the overturn of Sukarno the Russians lost heavy sums invested in Indonesia and have only slowly resumed their diplomatic and economic interest. In the last three or four years the Soviet Union has been trying to establish a mutual economic partnership with Japan. The bait is Siberia and a huge Japanese stake in investment and profits. Thus far the Japanese, with heavy U.S. involvements and looking some day to revival of trade with China, have been reluctant.

More recently Soviet economic and political efforts have ap-

peared in Southeast Asia—trade pacts with Malaya, based on
rubber; an increasing interest in Singapore; a drive to establish
relations with the Philippines; an expanding business with Thailand.

Few diplomats are more active than the Rusisans in East
and Southeast Asia. They have sent to Japan one of their most
attractive and able young diplomats, Oleg Troyanovsky, son of
a one-time Soviet ambassador to Japan and to the United States,
who was born in Japan and raised and schooled in the United
States and who often interpreted for Nikita Khrushchev and important Russians in their travels to the West and meetings with
Western statesmen. The Soviet Embassy in Tokyo has become
one of the most popular in Japan.

But this is not all.

The Russians have launched a curious cat-and-mouse game
with Taiwan. Unofficial Russian emissaries have visited Nationalist China for the first time since the rupture of relations in 1949.
Laudatory articles about Taiwan have appeared in the Russian
press, pointing to Chiang Kai-shek's achievements and to the
Russian background of Chiang Ching-kuo, Chiang's son and heir
apparent.

Speculation has been stimulated whether Moscow and Taipei might not contemplate, each for its own reasons, a renewal
of contacts and establishment of diplomatic relations. Memories
are recalled of Moscow's long and friendly association with
Chiang and the long and unfriendly relationship with Mao.
Might not the two sides have a sound basis now for re-establishing the old friendship? Possibly the politics of rapprochement are
beyond either side, but the prospect is enough to cause angry
thrills in Peking. If Peking could be provoked into breaking diplomatic ties with Moscow the Russians would win another string
for their propaganda bow. Even if Peking does not respond publicly, the idea of a flirtation between Chinese Nationalists and
Moscow Communists might cause discomfort. The calculated

publicity given to the Taipei-Moscow contacts seemed more like a war of nerves than a serious diplomatic exploration.

The Soviet effort in Asia has been broadened by Premier Brezhnev's proposal for a collective-security pact for Asia. He advanced the idea at the June meeting of Communist powers in Moscow and Peking promptly responded by calling him "the faithful disciple" of the late John Foster Dulles.

The epithet seemed more fitting than some Peking has used because, in effect, Brezhnev was picking up where Dulles left off. Dulles was the architect of the Asian security system, the network of ramshackle alliances, the SEATO and CENTO pacts, which were designed to "contain" China just at NATO was designed to "contain" Russia. Dulles' old pacts have just about run their course, and perhaps that is why Brezhnev decided to try to fill their place.

Brezhnev did not spell out what he meant, but Soviet commentators suggest that it is the replacement of the outworn U.S. alliance system which the Russians have in mind. They have mentioned as possible members of the security bloc: India, Pakistan, Afghanistan, Burma, Cambodia, and Singapore. Presumably Mongolia could be counted upon to join, already being bound by a defense treaty to Russia. Moscow would doubtless be pleased to the adherence of North Vietnam and North Korea, although neither is likely to sign up in view of the delicacy of their relationship to China.

The pact would provide a vehicle by which Moscow might win the signatures of the Eastern European countries which thus far have blocked an extension of their Warsaw obligations to the Far East. Within the framework of a general Asian pact their objections might be reduced. Japan would be a possible signatory, although it would be unlikely in the context of her relationship to the United States.

Moscow might be hoping to enlist not only Asian states and Communist states but also such a country as the United States in order to establish in Asia a counterpart of the often-discussed merger of NATO and the Warsaw Pact countries. Nothing has so infuriated the Chinese as this Soviet diplomatic gambit. Premier Chou En-lai called it "a new step taken by social-imperialism in its intensified efforts to rig up a new anti-China military alliance."

"This so-called Asian 'regional economic cooperation' is nothing but a trap for setting up a military ring of encirclement against China," he added. The Chinese have vented their anger not only against Moscow but against India (which actually has mixed feelings about the proposed pact). The Chinese theme is simple: Russia is trying to organize all Asia into one bloc of encirclement against China and at the same time to convert Asia into a region of economic exploitation. The Chinese are convinced that Russia and the United States are hand in glove in this; that the Russians are moving in with the relaxation of American influence in Asia so that henceforth the two powers may share hegemony in the continent.

But Peking believes that Russia is not only engaged in a diplomatic offensive with the Asian powers. The Chinese have seized upon remarks made by Premier Kosygin in his most recent visit to New Delhi about the desirability of a "land route" between Russia and India. This is viewed as a move by Moscow to open up a convenient method by which the Russians and the Indians can collaborate in military operations directed against such isolated and mountain-protected areas as Tibet. What Peking really fears is that Russia and India will make a pact under which they will jointly share China's Central Asian dependencies.

Weight is given to the Chinese suspicion by Soviet propaganda which is now being directed against the "oppressed minorities" in China. Just as Peking is showing solicitude toward the peoples of Russia's Baltic areas, the Ukraine, and Central Asia, so Moscow has launched propaganda broadcasts to the Mongols of Inner Mongolia, the Tibetans, the Kazakhs and Uighurs of

Sinkiang province. All of these peoples, in the view of Moscow radio, are being held in cruel subjection, deprived of human and national rights. The Moscow broadcasts could be employed by Radio Peking with a mere shift of names and places.

The Russians and the Chinese have erected enormous wireless transmitters beamed to each other's peoples, particularly minority peoples. The programs blast out twenty-four hours a day with tremendous volume. Anyone in the Far East or Asia turning on his shortwave radio finds the set vibrating from the volume of Chinese and Russian broadcasts and counterbroadcasts. Each side has set up jamming establishments which make those formerly used against the Voice of America seem like kindergarten installations. This is the big time. It has turned the Far Eastern airwaves into a cacophony of caterwauling.

The most important target of Soviet propaganda is the Uighur minority in China's westernmost province of Sinkiang, a province to which Moscow contends China's title is dubious. The campaign is led by Zunun Taipov, a former officer of the so-called East Turkestan Republican Army, once a Chinese Army general officer. The "East Turkestan Republic" was a short-lived Soviet-sponsored regime in Sinkiang which dissolved when the Chinese Communists came to power in 1949. Taipov is now in Moscow. He is the author of articles and broadcasts charging the Chinese with oppression of the Uighur nationals in Sinkiang and the Kazakh and Kirghiz minorities as well.

Soviet analysts depict the situation in Sinkiang as a struggle for power between supporters of Mao and Lin Piao, on the one hand, and the local population and regional leaders, on the other. Moscow names Wang En-mao, long-time commander of the Sinkiang military district, as being unsympathetic to Peking and has contended that Lin Piao plotted, apparently with some success, to reduce Wang's influence.

Moscow has displayed special interest in the situation in Yunnan province, bordering on Burma, in Tibet, and in Inner

Mongolia. In each of these areas Soviet propagandists maintained that struggles for power between forces supporting Mao and those opposed to him have been in progress, centering for the most part within the People's Liberation Army.

Just as Radio Peking has raised the banner of rebellion within the Soviet Union itself, so Russia and her allies are carrying the fight inside China. Moscow has contented itself, basically, with appeals to national minorities. Premier Tsedenbal of Mongolia goes further. He has promised to carry the fight against Mao into China itself, a pledge which means the supoprt of diversionary activities, subversion, and, potentially, of anti-Mao revolution.

There is hardly an area of imperialistic and militaristic activity which Russia and China have not mobilized against each other. Another charge against Moscow by Peking is that the Russians have embarked upon "gunboat" diplomacy. They point to the increase of Soviet naval operations in the Far East, conducted not only from the traditional base of Vladivostok (which the Chinese never refer to; they call it by its Chinese name of Hai-shenwei—presumably by way of indicating their prior claim to Russia's principal Pacific naval station) but from the Red Sea and the Indian Ocean. Russia, Peking claims, has signed a secret naval agreement with India giving her the right to base vessels in India in return for assistance to India against China. The Russians are said to have secret understandings with the Japanese under which passage of their naval craft through the straits of Soya, Tsugaru, and Tsushima are facilitated in return for economic concessions.

Thus, says Peking, the Russian fleet has obtained a new area of maneuver from the Kuriles to Taiwan, replacing the U.S. Seventh Fleet as the chief target of Chinese propaganda.

To Peking and Moscow the conflict has marched well past the preliminary phase. Before the end of summer in 1969 the residents in Peking and other Chinese cities were being exhorted

to save food and make sacrifices in preparing the country more
fully for war. Diplomats reported widespread rumors that the
government had begun to build up massive grain stocks in event
of Russian attack. Chinese troops were being shifted to the northeast, and civil defense and popular military training were being intensified.

On the Soviet side the new Mongol Defense Minister was
flying into Moscow for consultations. There were rumors that the
conflict might start with a Mongol-Chinese confrontation in which
Russia would then move to the aid of her small Central Asian
ally. In the Soviet border provinces of Kazakhstan and Uzbekistan the local populace was reading flamboyant declarations in
the press of the determination of Soviet border forces to protect
the fatherland at all cost, to maintain "peace" no matter how hard
the Red Army was compelled to fight the foreign invader.

The atmosphere had begun to take on an aspect only too
familiar to those who had watched the evolutionary path of Hitler's threat to Europe in 1937 and 1938. In the late 1930's efforts
were still in progress to halt the outbreak of general European
war. But more and more Europeans became convinced that conflict had become inevitable.

Today both Peking and Moscow use the Hitlerian analogy.
Peking sees the Kremlin as the new Reichschancellery. In Moscow Mao is seen as a metastasis of both Hitler and Stalin.

"There is only one explanation," a brilliant Russian scholar
said early in 1969. "Mao is mad. That is why he is so dangerous."

The young Russian went on. The worst thing, he said, was
that Russians knew how terrible it was to have a madman at the
helm. They knew the full horror of both Hitler and Stalin.

"We know now that Stalin was mad," he said. "But we know,
too, how many people believed him. That is what terrifies us
about Mao. We know he is mad. He must be mad. But how many
people believe him!"

CHAPTER XIII

Is War Inevitable?

The decisive question about Russia and China, the overriding question so far as their own people and the world are concerned is the simple one: Is war inevitable?

The quick answer is: No.

But it must immediately be qualified. If events are permitted to continue on the present pattern war *will* become inevitable. In measurable odds the chances of war between Russia and China have risen year by year in the past decade. Not always by the same amount and not regularly—there have been ups and downs, zigs and zags—but the tendency has been toward militarization of the conflict.

One factor which could radically shift the odds would be Mao Tse-tung's death. The possibility would then exist of a sharp turn in Chinese policy—away from hostility toward Moscow, away from a chauvinistic attitude toward the Soviet leadership, away from the view of Russia as a "renegade capitalist regime" and back to détente and the controlled collaboration of the early years of the Sino-Soviet alliance.

Whether a shift in Chinese policy is likely or possible with Mao's death has been debated within the Soviet Politburo. If such a change were likely, prudence might counsel patience, a vigilant military posture, and hope for a great transition after Mao's death. Moscow's counsels are divided. Some senior Politburo members believe a change in China can be expected. Younger members (none is younger than fifty!) and the military take a less sanguine view. They are not certain that the opponents of Mao's policy (the *real* Communists, as they like to call them) will come to power. By the time of Mao's death men like Liu Shao-Chi and others in whom Moscow has more confidence may have been executed or so politically discredited that there would be no realistic hope of their coming to the top. Many in Moscow feel that Mao and his "clique" have grasped power so firmly that even if Mao dies he will be succeeded by someone of identical ideas—that is, by Lin Piao, his designated heir, who the Russians believe not only holds views like Mao's but who inspired and encouraged Mao in the Cultural Revolution and the deepening anti-Russian orientation of Peking's policy.

Against this there must be cited the analogy of Stalin's Russia. Before Stalin died on March 5, 1953, it was universally believed by diplomats that his death would bring no real change in Soviet policy. Stalin had been in office so long, he had so repeatedly purged his Politburo, he was so closely surrounded by men of his own choice picked precisely because they believed exactly as he did, that the notion that his death would cause basic realignment in Soviet policy was unthinkable. Almost the only dissenter was George Frost Kennan, who had been declared persona non grata as American Ambassador to Moscow two years earlier because he had too deep and penetrating an understanding of the Soviet Union. Kennan believed Soviet change not only was possible but inevitable. He was laughed at.

The consensus about post-Stalin Russian policy proved totally wrong. Stalin's heirs stumbled over each other in their haste to switch and take positions opposite to those which they had so firmly and repetitiously pronounced.

Soviet policy changed after Stalin. Not only did it relax internally, but a strong drive arose toward amelioration of international tensions, toward détente with the United States (interrupted on occasions such as the Cuban missile crisis), toward rationalization of Soviet relations with many countries and on many issues.

Thus it would be dangerous to overlook the possibility that Mao's death could bring a sharp turn in Chinese policy, a switch back toward a line of arms-length collaboration with Moscow, a deliberate relaxation of border tensions, in ideology, and in relations with other Communist parties, an effort to minimize rather than maximize frictions.

Such a right-angle turn in Chinese policy could melt the rigidity in Sino-Soviet relations. It could restore the Sino-Soviet alliance as a major factor in the world balance of power and inaugurate a new era of Russian-Chinese collaboration directed against the rest of the world and, specifically, against the United States. It would confront the United States with the most critical foreign policy crisis of the century—the prospect of facing 1 billion to 1.2 billion Chinese and Russians armed with nuclear weapons in bewildering array, the latest in modern military technology, striding the Euraslan supercontinent like a colossus.

The prospect is chilling and it is precisely this dreadful potential which has caused Americans to welcome Sino-Soviet hostility. The possibility of a Sino-Soviet détente should not be overlooked, because it is the sudden, the unexpected, the nonlogical, it-can't-ever-happen events which change the course of world history.

But the odds against a rapprochement are long. When it is recalled that at the moment when Russia and China had most to gain from their alliance (at the height of the cold war) Stalin went on scheming and plotting against Mao; when it is recalled that at the moment of Russia's greatest breakthrough in missile-rocket-nuclear technology in 1957–58 she refused to back China in a challenge of the United States; when it is recalled how global, how tidal is the momentum of the present conflict, with its pervasive spread into almost every human activity, it becomes obvious that it would not be easy, even in a totalitarian state, to send the whole apparatus into reverse. Not impossible. But extremely difficult.

The fact is that Soviet policy has been moving on a broad front to meet every necessity of conflict with China. This has not been confined to deployment of troops and emplacement of weapons, Party polemics, the propagandizing of the masses and preparation of public opinion for the coming war, the moves to line up allies and seize the commanding diplomatic ground in Asia.

The most important moves have been designed to secure the Soviet flank in Europe and to neutralize the United States or, at best, to win it as a partner against China.

The 1968 Czech crisis revealed several facets of the Soviet outlook. Czech liberalism threatened the Kremlin effort to contain Soviet liberalism. If Czechs could speak, write, read, meet, and travel freely it would be difficult to hold back demands in Russia for these fundamental human rights. If Czechs achieved these liberties the other peoples of Eastern Europe would demand them. In no time the existing tendencies toward diversity in Eastern Europe would erupt in what the Kremlin considered a kind of anarchy in which Communist-governed peoples would possess the right to protest, to diverge, to vote, and even to expel Communist governments from office. Not many men in the Politburo could feel confident of holding power in the face of such freedoms.

Beyond the questions of human spirit and political principles there was another even more compelling—the threat the Czechs posed to the Warsaw Pact, to the whole painfully constructed Soviet security glacis, the reverse *cordon sanitaire* which was Stalin's chief postwar creation in Europe.

The Czechs contended that they had no intention of leaving the pact, but as seen by the Kremlin and its generals no matter what the Czechs said liberalization did threaten the pact. After Prague fell Budapest and Warsaw would tumble. Bucharest was already shaky. East Berlin could not withstand such a cataclysm. The whole protective East European shield would crumble and the real Russian nightmare would be ushered in—the renaissance of Germany as Europe's greatest power and that most terrible of threats, German revanche.

And all this at a moment of extreme and gathering danger in the East. To the Soviet generals this presented the threat of two-front war, of an opportunity for Germany or less-than-loyal Eastern Europeans to take advantage of Soviet preoccupation in the Far East to raise questions, threats, to demand territorial revisions.

The arguments of the Soviet military for quick, harsh action to preserve the status quo in Czechoslovakia and in the Eastern Europe defense zone would have carried the day even if the specter of Russian liberalization had not already haunted Brezhnev and Kosygin.

Czechoslovakia, in a sense, was the first victim of impending war in the Far East.

Fear of European repercussions at a moment when Moscow is preoccupied in the Far East has not lessened. In 1969 it took the form of Soviet diplomatic efforts to improve relations with West Germany, to defuse the West German threat by establishing a new groundwork for collaboration between Bonn and Moscow. It was being pursued in many ways and not always at first hand by Soviet diplomats. By a touch of irony, at the very time when the Russians were wooing Bonn they professed to see efforts by the Chinese to establish a special relationship with West Germany. In reality the tenuous Chinese-German contacts were a direct outgrowth of the Soviet economic blockade of China. Peking was trading with Düsseldorf and Hamburg not because of a desire for better Chinese-German relations but because Moscow would not trade with Peking.

In fact, Germany is only a part of the picture—the Russians are making every effort to improve their general relationships in Western Europe against the day when the Far Eastern crisis deepens.

Overshadowing all of this is the persistent, broad, and pervasive effort by Moscow to settle outstanding questions with the United States.

This policy probably has roots going back to Khrushchev's ill-starred attempt for rapprochement with Eisenhower in 1959–60, when China's malevolent attitude toward U.S.-Soviet friendship was made bitterly apparent.

The Soviet drive has picked up momentum in the past two years. It has followed the line so often urgently whispered by Russians, unofficially and officially, to Americans that Soviet-American issues should be resolved because of the growing menace of "those people." The strength of the Soviet move in this direction began to be evident in the final months of the Johnson administration. Only the intractable Czech crisis prevented a summit meeting of President Johnson and Premier Kosygin at Leningrad or Moscow and a full-dress effort to resolve the major issues of nuclear arms, proliferation, disarmament, and, quite probably, Western Europe.

The Johnson-Kosygin initiative was put aside by both sides with deep reluctance. But with the coming to office of President Nixon, American rapprochement has moved forward again to number-one priority on the Soviet agenda. It holds a very high rank on Mr. Nixon's agenda as well.

The Russian drive was stimulated by an almost paranoid fear that the United States might turn up in China's corner. When a Russian suggested this to me for the first time a couple of years ago I burst out laughing. The vision of President Johnson and Chairman Mao sitting down over a cup of tea seemed too ridiculous. My Russian friend was offended. It was no laughing matter, he said. The Russians knew all about the secret talks the United States was having with the Chinese "in the back room of that Hong Kong bar."

Soviet concern over U.S. rapprochement with China was apparent after President Nixon's election. A succession of unofficial and quasiofficial Russians appeared in New York and Washington. They wanted to know, of course, what the new President's policy would be toward the Soviet Union. They were especially eager to learn what they could about "these rumors we hear of the possibility of a new approach by Washington to Peking."

The intensity of Soviet concern over U.S. relations with Peking is an eloquent measure of the importance they attach to the position of the United States as tension deepens in the Far East and the real risk of war increases. The Russians are well aware that if the United States takes their side or stands on the sidelines the strength of Russia's position will be tremendously strengthened.

Thus regardless of genuine concern by the Russians for resolution of critical arms questions with the United States, the China issue is the real denominator and motivating factor in the Moscow diplomatic posture. So strong is the Soviet urge toward keeping the United States out of Peking's camp that, even at a moment when Moscow authorities are intensifying their restrictions at home (in the guise of strengthening the home front because of the "war danger" in the Far East) and embracing American correspondents within the scope of higher security barriers, they display to American diplomats nothing but friendliness and consideration. On the official level Americans and Russians seldom have gotten on so well.

China has not matched Russia's diplomacy. By the time the ninth Party Congress convened in April 1969 she had virtually cut herself off from diplomatic or any other contact with the world. Her ambassadors had been summoned home (except for one, the ambassador in Cairo), her diplomatic missions were down to a few duty officers, most of her newspaper correspondents had been brought back to Peking, she had few trade officials left abroad. Virtually no foreigners of any kind were being admitted to China.

China has not been so isolated from the outer world since before the Europeans battered down the doors of the port cities in the early nineteenth century.

As far as the United States is concerned there have been one or two tiny signals: a suggestion for a renewal of ambassadorial meetings in Warsaw (quickly canceled); a few hints at diplomatic receptions in Peking; a speech by a Foreign Office official saying that there were no basic conflicts between the United States and China—only the Formosa issue, and that had arisen after the Korean war, which had been started by the Russians. The implication of all this is that the Russians have deliberately sought to make Chinese-U.S. relations impossible, a theory which may well have some validity.

Each time the United States has attempted some small step such as minuscule relaxation of restrictions on trade and travel, the Chinese have resolutely turned their faces away. Thus far they are not convinced that the United States genuinely desires better relations. They see the U.S. moves as gambits to lull China into letting her guard down, and then, when China's security is relaxed, Russia and the United States confronting China with an ultimatum she would be compelled to yield to. After the ninth Party Congress the Chinese began painstakingly restaffing their diplomatic missions. It is possible that as tensions rise in the Far East they might, sooner or later, play the diplomatic card. It seems dubious that they would like to see the United States aligned with their enemy, but to the Chinese rapprochement involves great difficulty. It is their propaganda line—possibly believed by the Chinese leadership—that, in fact, the United States and Russia are working in a strange alliance against China. To move toward some new, more friendly, more rational relationship with the United States would not be so easy.

The American position toward the Russo-Sino conflict remains to be spelled out. Many Americans view conflict between Russia and China or even all-out war between Russia and China as a boon to the United States, a clash between hostile Communist giants which could only weaken both contestants and strengthen the United States. Their attitude is similar to that expressed by President Truman (then still a senator) when the Nazis attacked Russia: Let the two dictators, Stalin and Hitler, fight it out.

But the problem of Russo-Sino war is too complex and dangerous to be dismissed by saying "A plague on both their houses." It would almost certainly be a nuclear conflict—the first major use of these weapons in mankind's history. No one can be certain what the consequences would be, but certainly the fallout from the Chinese and Russian bombs would be deposited on North America and the United States, probably in amounts more deadly than would fall elsewhere on the earth (except at the site of the explosions), with the exception of Japan; the prevailing wind currents of the earth would attend to that.

Both China and Russia are known from their tests to use very "dirty" bombs—weapons producing great quantities of fallout—and this is particularly true of the Chinese bombs. The fallout could be expected to be not only extensive but extremely dangerous.

This would be disaster enough. But the prospect that China and Russia could fight a mass war on the Asian continent without dragging other Asian powers, willy-nilly, into the conflict seems unrealistic. India, already in a de facto state of war with China, would be involved. The question of Japan quickly would become more critical than the Japanese seem to realize, as the fallout rained down. Where would Southeast Asia stand? North Vietnam? North Korea? Hong Kong? Or even Formosa, flirting with the Russians but standing with the Chinese Communists on territorial issues? Would Eastern Europe be drawn to Russia's side in spite of itself? Much depends on the success of the Russian effort to patch together an Asian security pact. Certainly the signatories to such a document would be participants in the war.

Seen in realistic terms it does not seem that the Russo-Chinese conflict is one the United States can lightly brush aside. The stakes are too great—for our own interests and for those of our friends. The United States is the number-one power in the world. Number two and number three cannot fight without radically affecting the power balance in Asia and Europe and in the world. The United States has an interest in every part of it.

All of this puts to one side the humanitarian aspects of so vast a war and the moral responsibilities of American leadership.

The question thus is posed as to what would constitute positive American policy and how it might be advanced: Is it to the advantage of U.S. national interest to side with Russia, with China, or with neither? What elements in the situation might be employed to advance both U.S. and world interests?

The first factor which strikes even the most casual analyst is that the United States, with its enormous military, political, economic, and social power, is the only world force capable of exerting the influence which can affect the outcome of the conflict and which might prevent its outbreak. No other combination of powers, even if unified, would be likely to exert major influence on two countries of the magnitude of Russia and China.

However, the United States is not in a favorable tactical situation to affect the conflict because of the fact that American relations exist only with one participant—the U.S.S.R. Outside of ritualistic diplomatic meetings at Warsaw, sometimes suspended for a year or two, there are no diplomatic contacts between the United States and China.

If the United States is to take a serious role in the Sino-Soviet dispute it must establish a viable relationship with China.

Even if, in the end, national interest dictated that we were better served taking the Soviet rather than the Chinese side, we would radically improve our bargaining position if a genuine possibility existed of a détente with China.

To some the possibility of a real change in relationship with China seems an insuperable barrier. But, in fact, a creative approach has not been foreclosed. The Chinese themselves have several times hinted at a useful first step: a simple American declaration, made in the light of certain understandings, that the fate of Formosa is a Chinese question, one which must be resolved by the Chinese themselves.

Action on Formosa almost certainly must be the first step in any shift of U.S. relations toward China. It is the first and sometimes the only impediment mentioned by Peking. The virtue of the simple declarative formula that Formosa is a Chinese question to be resolved by the Chinese is that it expresses a principle on which both Nationalist China and Communist China agree. Both regard Formosa as part of China. Both believe that the Chinese and only the Chinese should settle questions regarding China.

As far as the United States is concerned this would not move into new and unprecedented ground. It would merely be a return to the position we held prior to the outbreak of the Korea war. It was Korea which poisoned American relations with China; which caused us to place Formosa under our protection; to ban trade and travel to China; to organize an economic blockade of China; to ban Communist China from the United Nations; to deny her diplomatic relations.

The other virtue of the simple declaration about Formosa is that it would not spell out the future. It would not specify procedures. It would not even define who is Chinese and who is not. Taipei could define the formula one way, Peking another, and Washington a third. So long as no one tried to define it precisely it could be accepted by all three.

The next question engaging Communist China is that of "American bases" on Formosa and the use of the Seventh Fleet to protect the island against invasion. Here time and circumstance could provide a relatively simple approach for the United States. Long since any large-scale American forces have vanished from Formosa. The island is employed only as a secondary land and air-staging point for Vietnam. Naval facilities are minor. The United States could abandon its remaining facilities on Taiwan without a material effect on its strategic position in the Pacific. There would remain the Seventh Fleet and the question of American response in event of an attack on Taiwan from the mainland, but some specialists feel it would not be difficult to resolve this question by a tacit understanding between Peking and the United States that there would be no attempt by forceful means to change the status of Taiwan in return for U.S. withdrawal of the protective mantle. Here the stumbling block would be Taiwan, fearing any change in its status as bringing nearer the possibly inevitable day of an end to Nationalist rule. But there would be room for negotiation with mainland China along lines of Peking's acquiescence in the indefinite continuance of the Taiwan regime once the principle of the island's indivisibility from China was established.

This does not exhaust the questions to be resolved with China. There are questions of economic blockade and travel, both representing an area in which U.S. power to maneuver is extensive. The blockade is largely archaic. China can purchase most of what she must have. It pinches most strongly on her export trade, limiting purchasing power by limiting ability to acquire foreign exchange. By a stroke of the pen the United States could restore most of China's trade. It is a lever of enormous value.

Chance and fortuitous development of circumstances place another tool in American hands. China has long charged that we have circled her with military bases; that together with the Russians and Indians we have ringed her frontiers with guns, planes, missiles, and warships.

Chinese fear focuses on U.S. action in Vietnam, which is viewed in Peking as the opening stage of U.S. war against China, the establishment of a reliable *place d'armes*, a complex of bases and airfields from which nuclear attack on China might be carried out.

The Vietnam war is obviously moving—if slowly—toward liquidation. Its end would effectively eliminate a cornerstone of China's indictment against American policy.

A lesser Chinese charge centers on Okinawa, which China calls a "stationary nuclear aircraft carrier" pointed toward China. Okinawa's status too is in a stage of metamorphosis. It is on the way back to Japanese control and Japan refuses to permit its use as a nuclear base.

This list comprises most of the Chinese case against the United States. It is not so difficult a list in 1969 as it appeared to be a few years ago.

Most persons begin their examination of U.S.-China relations with the question of establishment of diplomatic missions and Peking's representation in the United Nations. The question of formal relations hardly needs to be touched until the other thorny questions are resolved. If they could be settled, diplomatic relations would flow almost automatically.

However, positive action to remove barriers to U.S.-China relations should be viewed only as a step toward quite a different aim—the aim of maximizing U.S. influence in the Sino-Soviet dispute.

By eliminating barriers to diplomatic interchange with China the United States could make its influence felt in Peking and would acquire the ability to provide a counterweight to Moscow.

If Moscow believed that the United States had no choice but to take a neutral stand or side with her, our ability to influence Russian conduct would be limited. If Moscow knew a rapprochement between the United States and China could occur it should put the brakes on precipitous Soviet action.

But this merely constitutes "crisis management." It enables the United States to move to a central position of influence with both great countries. The question would then be: How could this weight be employed not merely to resolve the immediate conflict but to remove for the foreseeable future the possibility of nuclear disaster?

The great Soviet statesman Maxim Litvinov, who represented Russia at Geneva in the critical 1930's when the League of Nations was vainly struggling to halt the advance of World War II, cried again and again: "Peace is indivisible!" His eloquence did not stop Adolf Hitler but the truth of his declaration has echoed down the corridors of time. Peace is indivisible. If shattered in Asia by war between Russia and China it will not be put together again in our day—if, indeed, the world should survive.

No step which might prevent the outbreak of war should be overlooked. Action should not merely deter hostilities. It should utilize the crisis to create a solution which would place peace on a secure foundation.

This would be the great crowning contribution of American statesmanship. It should not be beyond the limits of American ingenuity, creativity, resources, and diplomacy.

There is an underlying instability on the continent of Asia, and it is not only the dangerous instability centering around the key relationship of Russia and China. Instability affects almost every political body in Asia. It is a continent in motion, set into rapid oscillation by the shattering effect of World War II and the destruction of the old colonial system. The life, politics, and economics of every Asian country have been affected. Most Asian countries have won statehood only in the last quarter century. The whole continent is still shaking as peoples, states, and philosophies seek some natural balance.

The situation is made more complex by age-old antagonisms:

the conflict between Indians and Pakistanis, between Vietnamese
and Cambodians, between Thais and Cambodians, between the
peoples of the high Himalayas and those of the lowlands (China
and India). Conflicts exist between new nations and minorities
within nations—the tribal feuds of northern Burma and those of
Laos, for example.

Superimposed on these historic antagonisms are those of recent vintage—the conflicts of sociopolitical origin: North versus
South Vietnam; North versus South Korea; guerrilla war in northeast Thailand and Nagaland.

Underlying all the conflicts, feuds, wars, rebellions, and
antagonisms can be found an economic infrastructure: the problem of population and of food. It is this problem which fuels the
intense hostility and chauvinism of China's attitude toward her
neighbors and notably her greatest neighbor, Russia. The same
problem affects India. It affects the relationship of Southeast
Asia with China. Southeast Asian states fear China may seize
them as a source of food. China fears the United States, by establishing a sphere of influence in Southeast Asia through the
Vietnam conflict, may place itself in a position to deny China
access to the rice of these rich food-surplus countries.

Regardless of steps to halt nuclear collision between Russia
and China, no peace will withstand a lengthy test unless it is
founded on a solution of the food-population crisis. Unless China
can find a way to feed this year's mouths and next year's and
those the year after, she will fight to get that food. The threat
of aggressive action if stayed, perhaps, in the northeast will simply be renewed in the southeast.

No resolution of the China crisis and the Asian crisis can be
expected without an answer to the food-population equation.

By good fortune we hold the key to the only answer. The
United States—with some collaboration by Canada, Australia,
and the Soviet Union—can feed China and the rest of Asia; can
guarantee that no Chinese baby will starve; can make certain

that China need not fight, north, south, east, or west to guarantee the survival of her population.

The United States possesses the most productive agricultural system the world has ever seen—so excessively productive that it is now running at less than a quarter throttle. For years farmers have been paid, coddled, and persuaded not to boost production because there was no market for what they could grow.

But at the same time tens of millions in Asia (and elsewhere) live on subsistence or starvation diets. China exists on the precipice of food disaster. One bad crop year would put her at the mercy of the world—unable to feed her people herself, unable to buy food to feed them. Soon even in good crop years she will face the same plight.

This overhanging danger can be removed unilaterally by the United States or by United States leadership in the creation of a world food pool on which food-deficit nations like China could draw, not as a matter of grant or benevolence or charity but as a *matter of right*.

The matter of right is the key. For if China must come cap in hand to do penance to the world, to beg forgiveness for a bowl of rice or a sack of wheat, she will not. Possibly the old China would. Not the new. She will fight first. If political conditions were attached to the provision of foodstuffs the scheme would founder on the hard rock of China's flaming nationalism. It might work with lesser states, unable or unwilling to face the military alternative. But there is no reason to suppose it would work with China.

This does not mean that the United States and its possible partners of Canada, Australia, New Zealand, and Russia would or should be compelled to guarantee progressive escalation of food production to meet an infinitely expanding Chinese population. By no means. There must be two positive provisions—both, fortunately, completely in line with present Chinese policy. One is that China take active, effective steps (and the same would apply to all countries drawing on the food pool) to hold population at existing levels and to use all technical aid which other states could provide to accomplish this task. This, hopefully, would enable China to stabilize her population not far over the billion mark (even with all the most costly and efficient of modern technical miracles it would take some time to reach all of China's child-bearing population).

China and other food-deficit states would assume a second obligation: that they maximize their own food production, drawing upon the best technological experience of the world.

On both points—population control and improved food-production technique—the world food pool would make available the best scientific expertise of the United States, Russia, and other countries.

It might be objected that China would not agree even to these positive proposals, but China already has population control and higher food production as national political objectives. Peking is doing what it can (with marked inefficiency) to hold down population. It is trying its best to grow more food. No major political or ideological barrier should exist to placing the program into operation once agreement on basic principles was obtained.

This program would cost money. American farmers must be paid for their wheat. They would not want domestic food prices depressed by quantities overhanging the market. But a two-price system with the U.S. government subsidizing, in part, the program for production for the world food pool would meet this need. Food-deficit states like China would not obtain food free of charge. They could pay their share, although not the full cost. Coupled with programs to increase China's foreign exchange earnings, the program could be financed within the bounds of present U.S. budget projections merely by diversion of fractions of the sums being spent on armaments.

The food-population program would not automatically solve

all of China's—or Asia's—problems. But if, as projected, Russian collaboration is made a basic requisite; if the United States by deed, word, and action made plain that no political pressures were to be attached to the pool, that it was to be drawn upon strictly as a basis of need by any and all nations, it would at a single stroke create a new community of world interest on which a viable structure of peace and security could be erected. If the great powers worked together to feed each other, to meet the most critical problems of population pressure without border conflict or nuclear war, a framework would be established in which the environment of mutual aid, assistance, and confidence —rather than the reverse—could grow and strengthen.

What, then, of the great "problems" of communism—the wars of liberation, China's frontiers, Moscow's ideological competition, the complex of banal and boring issues which make up the small change of daily rhetoric in *Pravda* and the *People's Daily*?

It would be naïve to suppose that this superstructure of hate and passion would immediately melt in the warm glow of well-filled stomachs and people no longer burdened with the intolerable survival problems. But, in the wise words of Maxim Litvinov, "peace is indivisible." If the world could make such great progress, under American leadership, it would begin to gain the confidence and experience to cope with relatively smaller, more simple problems which inevitably would persist and arise anew every day.

It does not seem utopian to suppose that a resolution of the Russo-Chinese crisis would give the superpowers on which the burden of responsibility for maintenance of world peace primarily rests the initiative for positive solution of other problems. If two nations as antagonistic as Russia and the United States in the worst of the cold-war days could emerge from the brink of nuclear crisis with a clear sense of responsibility for mutual collaboration in the interest of survival there can be no reason for total pessimism over the Sino-Soviet conflict.

The present dangers of war between Russia and China are demonstrably great. Equally demonstrable are the opportunities for American leadership to transform the world, moving it from the brink of destruction to an environment in which men and women of all nations, all races, all kinds of politics, could live in peace and security.

It hardly seems possible that an America imbued with a tradition of leadership, of moral responsibility, possessing the world's greatest pool of creativity, know-how, and technique, will not muster every strength to avert potential global suicide.

The opportunity for the United States, for its President, for its national leaders, for its ordinary citizens is one which has not been equaled in the nearly 200 years of the Republic's existence. Grasped with imagination and vigor, it could preserve for another 200 years the American dream. Fumbled it could mean death of the dream in the holocaust that looms over the empty steppe from which Genghis Khan and his destroyer battalions once set out to conquer the known world, to destroy its achievements, and to kill its men. But this time not even a pyramid of skulls would survive to mark man's final act.

Index

HARRISON E. SALISBURY probably knows Russia better than any other living American correspondent, having traveled widely and frequently through almost every part of the Soviet Union, including the long-sealed-off regions of Siberia, the sub-Arctic, and Central Asia as well as the Volga country and the Ukraine. He has also covered the entire periphery of China, traveling more than 25,000 miles along China's frontiers from the jungles of Southeast Asia to the bristling Siberian-Chinese border.

His first assignment in Russia was as head of the United Press bureau in Moscow in 1944. After joining *The New York Times* in 1949 he became their Moscow correspondent and remained there for the next five years. Out of his observations during this period grew his celebrated series for the *Times*, "Russia Re-Viewed," which brought him the 1955 Pulitzer Prize. He subsequently wrote two books dealing with the same period, *American in Russia* (1955) and *Moscow Journal — The End of Stalin* (1961). His recently published *The 900 Days: The Siege of Leningrad* was widely acclaimed and an important best-seller.

As a result of his reports Mr. Salisbury was barred from Russia for five years, and was not allowed to return to the country until 1959. At that time he stayed for nearly six months, traveling thousands of miles within the Soviet Union. His 1960 book, *To Moscow and Beyond*, was a result of this trip. He has since revisited Russia in 1961–62, 1966, 1967, and 1969.

Mr. Salisbury was born in Minneapolis in 1908 and was educated in the public schools there and at the University of Minnesota. He is Assistant Managing Editor of *The New York Times* and lives in New York City with his wife.

(Continued from front flap)

relations between the two great Communist parties, from the days of Borodin through the Stalin and post-Stalin periods. He discusses past Russian campaigns in Central Asia and the Far East and the more contemporary conflicts, political, ideological, and military. He describes the forces in Asia which can be expected to be set in motion by this conflict, and he closes with a study of U.S. policy in the midst of this dangerous context.

Pulitzer Prize-winner Harrison E. Salisbury has here written a thoughtful, timely book. It is vital reading if we are to understand the basis of the Russian-Chinese conflict. America may be forced to pay attention sooner than many think.